THE **PACK**

PERILS AND PEACE OF NATURE

LAKE OF THE WOODS

C. LARSON

 **FriesenPress**

One Printers Way
Altona, MB R0G 0B0
Canada

www.friesenpress.com

ISBN
978-1-03-914019-6 (Hardcover)
978-1-03-914018-9 (Paperback)
978-1-03-914020-2 (eBook)

1. BIOGRAPHY & AUTOBIOGRAPHY, PERSONAL MEMOIRS

Distributed to the trade by The Ingram Book Company

DEDICATION

To those with a passion to learn from nature and to my husband
who never stopped believing in The Pack.

FOREWORD

My soulmate and I chose a remote location to seek life's truth through pioneering our homestead on a remote island in Lake of The Woods, Northwestern Ontario, Canada. There our Pack was confronted with obstacles and Natures law, 'Survival of The Fittest', forcing us to question our values to find out what really mattered.

My lifelong commitment to professional sport, having trained at the highest levels taught me to provide "uncompressing commitment to shared goals", and is the basis of my loving relationship with Connie. She has amazed me with the same gumption to commitment to life's values and truths. Her memoire illustrates how everyone can apply nature's lessons to their daily challenges.

Connie searches her soul and personal relationships. She lays them bare at her readers feet to apply to the many hurdles, using Mother Nature as her mentor. Living in nature, respecting it, experiencing it, served as our little Pack's plan to solve life's problems and to find our way through them.

With Sekima our malamute, his instinctual wisdom at our side, the heart felt adventures we endured strengthened our Pack and supported its success. You should read this story. Let The Pack reveal lessons learned from nature and how to apply them to your life's obstacles and challenges.

PRAISE FOR THE AUTHOR

The Pack is a multifaceted story about a special place that provides growth challenges, beauty, solitude, and adventure in a cherished natural part of our world. Some would argue that Lake of the Woods is the most beautiful place on earth.

In 'The Pack', respect for our natural world permeated the personal lifestyle and day to day life choices, responsibilities and tasks. 'The Pack' provides a unique, perspective on the world around us, minus many of the larger and more distant world issues. As the story unfolds you are transported to a different reality, one where you become part of the story, unsure of the outcomes. Will you survive the life threatening events and see another day? Will you experience injury with lifelong effects? Will the closeness to the natural world lead to more respect and educate us about the limits of our human capabilities? The personal memoir allows us to contemplate our existence on many levels. A thoroughly enjoyable read. As a first foray into the book world, thank you for taking us on your personal journey.

Sue Bruning, past President of Lake of the Woods Property Owners Association, (now Lake of the Woods District Stewardship Association)

PRAISE FOR THE AUTHOR

What would drive a person to leave civilization behind to find solitude among the jack-pine and frozen waterways of the Canadian Shield?

Connie has crafted the "Pack" to lay bare the journey of thousands of steps to get to where she really wanted to be, at peace knowing where she belonged. "The Pack" is an autobiographical telling of her story of living on a small island where she can retreat away from the noise of life and look inside to see what really matters.

When Connie was living in Edmonton and a part of a Toastmasters Club, she would always look for a hook in her speeches to capture our attention and impart a memorable message and she continues to do this with her first literary endeavour. From her descriptions of the beauty of the landscapes of the Lake of the Woods to the relationships that develop between those rugged individuals, wanting waifs and people that just want to survive a little longer and build connections to sustain them.

Join "The Pack" and see the beauty of solitude and the warmth of a simple life unfold before you!

Danie Hardie, Creative Communications Ltd
Past International Director, Toastmasters International

CONTENTS

CHAPTER 1

THE STORM

What seemed like the worst of it was only the beginning. Wind whipped around with purpose, slapping through the pine boughs, sending brittle birch branches flying. Dark fall clouds ran furiously overhead, keeping pace with frothy rolling waves that slammed the floating boathouse. Waves, relentless as they hit it, over and over.

For now, there was little that we could do but watch the fury of the gale from inside the cabin. The single pane windows gave us a clear view of the swelling lake and the boathouse. The back two corners of the boathouse were attached by heavy winch cables to some gnarly jack pines on the island's shore, and they appeared to be clamped securely enough. It was hard to imagine what was happening to the boathouse below the waterline as it heaved and bucked, the studded frame twisting like a pretzel. On the front corners, large chains connected to concrete barrels sat at the lake bottom, preventing the structure from crashing to shore. The pressure strained every bolt, link, and board as the wind and waves lifted and threw it about.

The storm bellowed noisily through the cabin. One of the spruce giants nearby gave a thunderous crash as its roots tore loose, and its body careened to the earth. The wind screamed, and in a momentous thrust sent crests of four-foot waves spewing in the air and spun the boathouse sideways. Cables strained and failed.

Connections broke, and the boat house pivoted on what remained. The rain came then, in torrents, sending pine needles and debris racing down the island slopes towards the lake.

Experience told us to wait out bad weather on Lake of the Woods; the big lake in northwestern Ontario was an opponent that neither tired nor had mercy. But sometimes the stakes were too high. In this case, we not only envisioned a forty-by-forty-foot boathouse smashed to pieces on rocks many miles from our island, but our boat and outboard motor with it. We could not let that happen. We deliberated, argued, and finally agreed.

The storm outside was deafening. Thunder growled loudly and giant spruce trees groaned. Lightning darted this way and that in rhythm with our fears. Jim made his way to the shoreline and the boathouse as I trailed at the top of the steep steps. There was a deafening snap. I reeled around in time to witness a large spruce tree split in two, landing not three feet away. Its heavy-laden top just missed the corner of the cabin roof as it thumped to the ground.

I delayed no longer. I hurried down the steep steps, crossing the ramp that still bridged the boathouse to shore. Jim was inside taking survey of the damage. The right cable lay limp in the water. It had probably broken first and the sudden snap forced the front chain on the right corner to break away. The one concrete barrel on the left corner was not adequate to hold the boathouse in place for much longer, but sufficiently strong enough that it remained intact for the time being. The wave action combined with the heavy weight of the boathouse had obviously bounced the concrete barrel along the lake bottom until it had gotten caught on a big enough boulder to hold it fast. How long would it hold up? When it did let go, the last cable holding to shore would follow quickly.

Four-foot waves were cresting the interior walls of the boathouse and mopping the deck. The boat was tied securely to four-by-four posts and was riding each wave. If the boathouse broke free, our boat would go with it.

"I can't get the boat out. If I put it into reverse in these waves, it will swamp," Jim yelled above the storm.

"What about the boathouse? It can't take much more. Can you reconnect?"

"NO way," he said firmly. "Not in this storm."

I can't take credit for the idea we came up with next. Not sure if Jim would either. But, as usual, between the two of us, we came up with something that just might work. We had both seen large metal flatbeds, barges, pushed by tugs not a quarter their size on this lake. Perhaps the boat could act like a tug did and push the boathouse into place.

The decking was greasy underfoot. Jim held onto one of the vertical four-by-fours, his foot on the side of the boat, steadying it, as I stepped in. The engine kicked into gear on the first attempt. I eased the throttle forward. He positioned himself at the doorway of the boathouse, sighting the shoreline, shouting at me to give the boat full throttle. It made me nervous. I pretended I was in open water, trying to get the boat on step at its full speed, and not tied to a dock. I could not hear the engine above the storm, only felt the vibration.

Jim stood in front of me through the open doorway, the shoreline beyond. He roared above the storm. "Give it more. Turn it to the right."

The storm was deafening. I felt powerless. I pushed the lever forward an inch.

Jim left the opening and was back to the boat, screaming at me. "You put that thing in full throttle. All the way. You hear me!"

I nodded. This was my first attempt at driving a boat. I hated mechanics. I had no understanding and envisioned the boat breaking free and running through the front of the boathouse and onto the rocky shore. I did it. Steady but full throttle.

Jim gave me a thumbs up from the opening. "It's working," he shouted.

I could see it now. The shoreline was slowly changing in front of me. We were moving the boathouse! I turned the steering wheel hard to the right, still full throttle. I could feel the boathouse turning, taking the pressure off the only secure barrel. The boathouse was finally perpendicular to the shore. It had been dangerously dangling like a door on one hinge. Using the boat, we had positioned it to take the burden off the one remaining joint. Jim waved at me to straighten the wheel, but I had already anticipated the move. All I had to do was straighten out the wheel and pull back on the throttle, recognizing the force required to hold us steady with the shore. We had managed the first step. Now we would wait it out until it was calm enough to reconnect, unless, of course, we ran out of gas first.

It was times like this that affirmed our decision to leave the corporate world was the right one. The harsh northern Canadian climate tested everything that we had experienced in our lifetime. I knew for Jim—an ex-football player and an Eagle Scout, life could not get much better than this. This was not a practice game. This was the real thing. There were new dimensions, new challenges, and a whole life ahead of us that required new tackles, defenses, and strategies.

He had heeded his father's dying words: "Don't wait. Do it now while you still can." Here he was, living his dream. If it had not been for a failed life insurance physical and his skyrocketing blood pressure, perhaps the words would not have resonated. The world of sports was a double-edged sword. It had given him training for absolute focus, but it also meant there was no such thing as quitting. He had played the game, and lost. There were no more moves. He had given his all.

There is a time much later that he came to a conclusion as to whether he was premature with the innovative construction product, undercapitalized, or simply had too many lawyers on his Board of

Directors. It cost him family relationships and severe personal loss. It would likely take a long time before he believed that he had done everything to save relationships and his company. It would take much longer for him to reestablish family connections as he disappeared into the remote north to save his health and his soul.

For me, I had reached a personal high with a career in construction, owning my own renovation company. The company itself was doing okay—recognition awards and skinny profit, with a long road ahead. I had convinced someone with construction background to become my partner, as he was the perfect project manager—or so I thought. He had many great strengths, but sticking to the estimate was not one of them. He was caught stealing from one of our lumber suppliers, most likely to try to hide his failure. I lost respect and my admiration for him as a person. I wanted out.

I would miss my friends. They meant so much. Still, it was not enough. My heart just was not in it anymore. It was 1996. I was going to be forty soon, and there was an emptiness about my life. Relationships with males had been dead-end roads, and suddenly my mother, at sixty-three was taken away from me by lung cancer. She so desperately wanted to live. It seemed that she had just found a new beginning in her life that relieved economic hardships and allowed her to achieve independence. She liked to dance and sing; she was feeling joy when cancer struck. I sensed how precious life was, and that it would not wait for anyone.

Neither of us was impulsive. Neither of us anticipated that we would be making this decision this soon in our lives. Unlike the times in business or in our personal lives when we had decided to wait and see how things would turn out, this was different. Waiting did not seem to be an option. Mortality had struck quickly, bursting our lives like a rupturing abscess.

I longed to be in nature with a strong man, a man with character. Someone who would be there to share my dreams. I was born in a little log cabin, without water, without electricity; I longed to recreate a vision of my childhood, but without the hardship that my parents endured. I wanted to smell the pungent odor of a pine forest, the freshness in the air after a spring rain, baking bread, and venison stew. I wanted to float on my back in the lake's soft water and feel it caress my hair. I wanted to feel the strain on my muscles from working all day. I wanted to be back home in nature. I needed to feel that connection.

It is hard to imagine that this happens to everyone, at some time in life. Things seem to be heading in the right direction, and then, as the saying goes, the rug gets pulled out from under you. It could happen suddenly or it could be a slow process of ignoring and denying things that eventually add up to personal losses that take a long time to recover, or never do. The child that needs more and more before you realize they're an addict. The scandals that start small and blow into a movement. The infection that becomes sepsis. The continuous lies that are indistinguishable from the truth.

It could happen quickly. Illness strikes, you lose someone you love. *This is not happening to me; I am invincible.* But it is, and you are not. Isolation and fear. Worry and depression. Lost plans of a future that will never be created. My mother. His father.

Sometimes it is just waking up after many years, realizing that life is pretty meaningless; your senses are not acute, and your joyful memories are just that—memories—and they have faded and blurred. It was like that for both of us. We vowed we were going to do something about it before it was too late.

We both knew we had strayed from our path of being mindful, of inner joy, and our connection to the earth. We knew we had denied and rationalized. We knew that it would be a long road of recovery. We had physical and emotional wounds. We both believed that nature would heal those wounds. But sometimes, in order to heal, you have to make it through another storm.

CHAPTER 2

NOTHING MORE,
NOTHING LESS

Jim and I had been thrown together randomly in a golf tournament. By the third hole, we had more interest in each other than the golf game. That physical attraction, the curiosity and wonderment of magnetism that draws bodies together. We had plenty to talk about with similar industry backgrounds, but what lay underneath was temptation. Over the months, we talked regularly and saw each other infrequently. We were from different cities and our businesses were demanding.

When he offered to book a room next to his at a trade show that we were both taking part in, I hesitated. What did he want from me? So many times, men passed me by, believing I was untouchable. I did not understand how afraid they were of me, how threatening I had become in a male-dominated industry. Others were just there to take sexual pleasure and abandon me. I knew I could entice, tantalize, and seduce—but I could never enter a lasting relationship. Jim's confidence in his masculinity became a powerful draw. I said yes.

We had sex for the first time. Previously, when I connected with someone, it was simply for sex, an act filled with intense wildness, a way to let go of my troubled world. This was different. He was no doubt passionate, but he was also thoughtful and deliberate. He seemed intent to please, with a desire to be connected; whereas for me, because of a perverted past, I wanted to escape as quickly as I could. I needed complete control, I needed to bring a man to total abandon. Yes, I had initiated sex with him, but he was the one in control. He kept slowing me down, extending foreplay so that I had no choice but to relax and be present. He stayed with me for a while, and then left, leaving me wondering who this man really was—so different than anyone I had been with.

I was tired of the emptiness of my life. Occasionally, there were nice men that would do anything, and I felt nothing. More often, there were bad men I could not get enough of, men who would not commit. There were men that said they loved me, men that did not. Men I loved, but could not touch. I could not stand the pain of it anymore. One failed marriage of less than two years and countless superficial relationships. It was like riding a roller coaster that I could not get off of, one that I paid for at every twisted turn. There had to be more.

I stopped just going through the motions, and started questioning why my results were terrifyingly similar to the last. There was a long period of reflection, slowly and deliberately taking stock of my life. But now the waiting was over. I still did not understand why it was so critical to not delay, and others times necessary to wait. I was about to find out. Nature was about to teach me.

It had taken many years of developing ownership of who I was. The time had come. It had to be all or nothing. He was different enough. Over coffee the next morning, I gave my ultimatum. I wanted friendship without sex, or a committed relationship. Nothing more, nothing less. I had no more time to waste.

CHAPTER 3

AFTERMATH

Complete calm on the lake never lasted. Waves still churned into the boathouse opening, but the wind was only a light breath from the west. It had shifted direction, holding the boathouse in place without our assistance. It was a good time to reconnect the cables and see if there was any chance of fastening the concrete barrel.

Over an hour later, and with dusk fast approaching, we walked the perimeter of the cabin. All three of us. Our wolf-grey malamute cross, Sekima, had been left in the cabin on the first round with the storm. Now he trotted ahead of us, his impressive bushy tail curled tightly, intent on doing his own assessment. The boathouse was secure, at least for tonight. Nothing to do in fading light. I needed to get dinner started. Coal oil lanterns provided meagre light to the tiny kitchen. The small flame beneath the glass globe was little more than a candle's breath.

There were fallen branches everywhere. Several one-hundred-foot-tall spruce had toppled. They were bent in two with only the cores attached, arm size splinters still hanging on as though defying fate. The insulating foam board that Jim had been applying to the exterior of the cabin was still in place. There were no toppled trees on the roof. It could have been a lot worse. Everything could wait.

Sometime in the middle of the night, we awoke to a clap of thunder and howling winds. We were on high alert, drifting in and out of sleep, and then wide awake instantly. Using the flashlight next to the bedside, we made our way to the central room of the cabin to check on the boathouse. The light shone back at us from the reflection in the window. There was empty darkness around the halo of light that appeared like a full moon against the blackness of the night. We couldn't even see the tree that was just a few feet beyond. There was nothing except the howling. A flash of lightning lit up the sky. Just a glimpse, but there it was, a silhouette of the boathouse below.

CHAPTER 4

THE GAMBLER

The storm kept us up most of the night. I could not help but think how we had gotten here in the first place. How my path with Jim's was intertwined like braided ribbons. How as much as we struggled to be aloof, we were destined to bond. How our troubles became opportunities. It was a year or so, testing the waters, sharing and exposing our truths. I did not have total commitment. Instead, I had comfort. I had a relationship that felt like two people in a slow-moving canoe, paddling upstream, fluid strokes on a winding river, never quite knowing what was around the next bend.

As a get-away for us both, he had taken me on a trip to a place that was dear to him. We flew into Winnipeg, Manitoba and drove to a local resort on Lake of the Woods. It was early spring, with ice flows still on the lake. Our accommodations were tucked away below the main lodge, a large rock fireplace central to the open living, kitchenette, and dining area. The furniture was well worn, large couches and sagging leather, a tiny table with a yellow laminate top and chrome chairs.

We found an old deck of cards, and, with a bottle of Johnny Walker Black Label Scotch and a bucket of ice, we proceeded to play strip poker. I cheated, just a bit. I layered a few of my clothes. He made it to my underwear, and vice versa. And the last round, I won. We fell into bed laughing. We had left our corporate lives on the shelf, but for a moment.

The next morning, Jim had engaged a real estate agent to take us to an island that was for sale in Whitefish Bay. The ride on a windjammer was exhilarating, the ice boat with propellers in the back, just like they use in the Everglades, only skimming the surface of ice and water. The trapper's cabin, with its weathered reddish stained logs, looked stark and humble against the untouched snow and towering spruce. We meandered through forgotten trails to the southerly point of the island. It was the highlight. Ice dominated the large expansive view as far as we could see, dotted here and there with islands that bulged upwards beyond the flat landscape.

"Have you ever considered living on an island?" Jim asked on our return.

I shook my head. "No, I've never given it any thought. I don't know why someone would." We had discussed living in nature, but never an island.

"I have. I have been looking for close to ten years for an island in Whitefish Bay. It's the deepest, cleanest part of the lake. Nothing has come up until now."

He had been coming to this lake with his family since he was fourteen. I recognized how much it meant to him.

"Why don't you put in an offer?"

"It's a difficult time for me. The business requires so much of me, including all of the capital that I could muster."

"But this is the island you have always dreamed about having, is that not right?"

A sigh escaped him. "Yes. It's all I imagined. It's the right size. It's the right location. The cabin is not much, but it has character."

Somewhere on one of these islands, his father's ashes lay below a tree. I knew about his father's dying words. We had talked so many times of how much money it would take to disappear in nature.

I could not let it go. "Jim, this is it. What have you got to lose?

If he accepts your offer, you'll figure it out. I know that much of you already."

"I didn't know it was available until we got here. I didn't even bring a checkbook."

"So, do you want it? Is this what you really want? If it is, I have my checkbook. I can write a deposit for you. You can pay me back when we return."

I watched his big hands fold, and unfold, his face in deep contemplation.

"Are you sure? They might not accept my conditions but, like you say, what have I got to lose."

I knew by his earlier question—about whether I had ever considered living on an island—that he really did envision me being part of his life. It was the compelling conversations we had that always led us back to living in nature. I was not sure if he would include me in this journey, but I was certain that he would get there. I could not help but hear the lyrics of Kenny Rogers' "The Gambler." Jim certainly knew what it took to survive. Deep inside himself, Jim knew what to throw away and what was worth keeping.

He gambled, and I became part of it.

CHAPTER 5

STORMS COME AND GO

We were wary as the days went by. The old boathouse could easily hold two boats. It had a flimsy plywood exterior that acted as a perfect resistance as it struggled for position against westerly winds. It was too late in the season to attempt any modifications. The cables, the floating billets, the barrels and chains below, were old. Every storm brought further unease; every uneventful aftermath was a blessing.

There was significant reason for us to be up at the crack of dawn. There were fires to build and chores to do. It had been a restless night of anticipation and anxiety. It had been another violent fall storm. There was concern that the boathouse would break loose during the night, and anticipation that there was more damage to an already weary structure. To top it off, we were heading to Winnipeg for winter supplies. It was close to two hundred miles, and we hoped to make it back before dark. The fierceness of the storm was once again an imminent warning that winter was on its way.

Morning brought a view that was pleasing to the eye and provided tremendous relief. The boathouse was exactly where it should be. The day was overcast, but the stillness outside the window was serene. The lake was flat, untroubled by her dreams. She was deep sapphire in late fall. In the distance, towering spruce and pine framed the water's edge, a mass of random spikes jaggedly interrupting the dense cloud cover. They filled the horizon much like a mountain view as they followed the contours of the islands, valleys and humps, and towering spans of jaw-dropping enormity.

Jim started a fire in the small cookstove so that we could boil water for coffee. The dry Jack pine crackled as the flue gave it breath. We had made significant progress since making our small down payment on the five-acre island. The cabin had been fully furnished and equipped with everything needed for a summer vacation, but it had been late September when we took occupancy. This last month, we had worked from sun up to sun down getting ready for winter.

The used airtight heater we had purchased was inserted into the open granite fireplace that was central to the cabin. Jim's muscles had groaned over that 350-pound chunk of metal. It would keep us warm this winter. The granite fireplace was a good twelve feet wide and four feet deep, the open side of it facing the living space, the solid side backing onto the galley kitchen.

The gravity water system had been an old galvanized steel barrel outside, containing no more than fifty gallons. Jim had fabricated an indoor water system that needed to withstand plummeting temperatures. The barrel was now secured on a shelf tied to the kitchen side of the fireplace, as far-reaching upwards in the rafters as possible. It was optimal gravity that made the flow of water possible, and it was unlikely to freeze sitting next to the radiating heat from the warm granite. I remember, as a young child, looking at the skim of ice that would form overnight in the water pail. The water was so cold it made your teeth ache. I hoped that would just remain a young girl's memory.

Not yet tested, we had purchased a plastic line that had an inner collapsible tube. In theory, it would not freeze, as it would collapse when we pushed air through it using a bicycle pump. No water in the line. No water to freeze. We were prepared to sparingly use the water in the barrel and try to make it last a week, at which point we would hook up the line from the lake to the barrel using a small gas generator to provide power for the RV pump. We had already tested the distance. The 125 feet from the water to the cabin was doable, with a thirty-foot height. We used the same concept for the drain lines. Nothing or everything could go wrong. We anticipated that once the lake froze, we would have no gasoline delivery, and no propane delivery until spring. It was all based on best guess calculations on an ultra-stingy budget. Showers once a week. Dishes once a day, and no rinsing. Drinking water and water for coffee.

Some might be repulsed by such limitations, but how dirty can one get in the winter anyways? There would always be a pot of hot water heated on the hearth for light washing. In September, we had still been sweating most days as we tried to make ready for winter. We had been swimming daily in waters that were below 68°F. The leaves had turned, splashing sunshine yellow, blood red, and burnt orange, carpeted brilliance and random shades amidst a backdrop of giant Christmas trees and stately white and red pine. We swam as long as we could. There was no thinking. We dove in quickly.

It was definitely cold. It took several minutes to adapt. When windy, the water would be churned, driving colder water from the deeps to the surface. After a quick bath using biodegradable soaps, we scrambled up to the deck, our bodies shivering under thick bath towels. We let the sun kiss the goose bumps away as we relaxed on wooden deck chairs, watching the terns and loons gather in the channel. Sometimes it is necessary to do unpleasant things quickly. Do not wait.

I realized it was not always easy to do unpleasant things. I recalled my friend's behavior when she drank was nothing like when she was sober. I let it slide a long time and eventually I confronted her. It was destroying our friendship. Of course, she was stunned. Of course, she ended our friendship. I still feel badly. And yet, my most beautiful friendship to this day is when I did not wait. I plunged with an open heart, praying for mutual understanding.

Our indoor shower was manual, a black bag filled with warm water from the woodstove, raised to the rafters with a pully system. Each person had exactly five gallons to use in the fiberglass shower that was temporarily installed—save for the drain. The shower bag held as much water as is used in an older model flush toilet.

The outhouse was pre-existing—weathered barn board exterior with multiple layers of old shingles to its wavy roof surface and shifted hinges so that the door would not quite close. We kept a sturdy candle in the outhouse to save flashlight batteries. To keep the cheeks warm, we had cut a polystyrene foam insulation board to fit around the hole.

Cash was extremely scarce, but there was nothing wrong with our ingenuity and determination. We were resourceful, and Mother Nature would always find other lessons for us to learn. We thought we lived in a complex environment in the city. Both of us had chosen to be business owners, which in itself was challenging and often required adaptation to circumstances that were beyond our control. But day to day choices of what to eat, who to hang out with, or what to watch on television—that was simple stuff. At first glance, nature simply takes one's breath away, from the smallest of woodland flowers to the giant sequoias of California. And then you realize how ingenious and complex it all is, and how servile you are to its grandness. For all our planning and mindfulness, Mother Nature, in this remote wilderness, would constantly remind of us of our insignificance.

Gear packed we were ready to roll. We double checked for truck keys, wallet, and oversized cooler. We were picking up dry goods to take us to spring, and perishables that we hoped to replenish before ice-up. Round trip from the island without shopping was seven hours. We would have no time to spare.

The ramp was perfectly in position as we stepped across into the boathouse. Cheerfulness turned to alarm. Side ropes dangling into a pool of water. Boat stall empty. The red and white vinyl seats of the boat mirrored from below the water's surface, eight feet down. Motor submerged.

"Oh, no," I groaned.

"We must have gotten a big wave from the back." I could hear the anger rising in Jim's voice. He cursed our ignorance. We had been so preoccupied with getting ready for the long trip, we'd failed the basics. Boats needed to be parked with their bow out. Bow out meant it would ride the waves, not gulp a wave into the hull. It would have only taken a few big ones, and then she would have fallen below like a quickly deflating air balloon.

Hopeless. No phone. Seven o'clock on a brisk October morning, with only the odd hunter on the lake scouting for deer possibilities.

"What are we going to do?" I could hear the squeaky part of my voice as my throat constricted with apprehension.

"Either way, we have to get to town. The mechanic will tell us whether we have something to salvage."

"Do we forget about Winnipeg?"

"We don't know anything. We're up early enough that we have some time. You might as well go back inside. I'll sit on the shore to see if any hunters are out."

Jim sounded resolved. There really was no other choice. We had to get off the island. We had no way of sending a distress call. We had established no means of communication. No one was going to come looking for us.

I looked at the capsized boat. Every wrinkle in the seats, every gauge visible beneath the quiet water. I let the calm flow over me, let Jim's composure course through me.

"I'll bring you some hot coffee." I walked away, not wanting to continue looking at the wreckage.

The odds were not good that someone would miraculously show up, but short of setting the island on fire as a smoke signal, the best chance we had was to wait down on the shoreline until someone passed by.

We had settled in with hot coffee for a very long look at a neighboring island that sat some three hundred yards north of our position. We heard the rumble of a boat engine in the distance. The island across from ours was over two hundred acres that framed a lengthy, narrow passage to bigger waters. The boat was coming down the narrows. We set our mugs down, rose, and began waving our arms and yelling.

About a half hour later at the town's marina, the mechanic listened to our story. "The engine is completely submerged?" he asked.

The mechanic was a slight, short man. Greasy, thin hair matching greasy mechanic hands. A permanent half smile on his thin lips. Just normal features. Grey-green work pants. Light flannel checked shirt tucked in, neatly hiding a small belly. The mechanic seemed amused with the story. I knew by Jim's face he did not think it was something to be amused about. He moved closer to the mechanic. I was not sure if it was deliberate or not. Jim could make many men uncomfortable with his size. He shadowed the mechanic.

"Always, park bow out on this lake. One rogue wave can do it." There's that smile again.

"I won't be forgetting that any time soon. But tell me, what can be done?" I saw Jim glance at his watch, registering how many hours we had left.

"Should be no problem getting it off the bottom. You say there's only about eight feet of water in the boathouse?"

"I suspect so."

He explained that he and his son would take a run out to the island with a water pump. It was a good day for it. Nice and calm.

"Once we get it up even a bit, it won't take long. The key is drying it out. The motor will likely start but would be best if we bring it into the shop. Let it sit overnight in the heated garage to get rid of any water that could cause you problems later when it turns cold, which, by the way, it is. They're calling for 5°F by the weekend."

"Sounds great." I had anticipated much more. "Just like that?"

"Sure. Just like that."

Marina Joe's wife had come out of the back during the last minutes of our conversation. Dark eyes set back in a narrow face with sharp pointed nose. Plaid flannel shirt to match her husband's.

"Pleased to meet you, Mr. and Mrs. Larson. Name's Nora. Sorry to hear about your plight."

I offered an extended hand. I did not bother telling her we were not married. "Your husband's going to perform a miracle." My disposition had suddenly become much brighter. Jim was looking to leave.

"I heard you have no phones, and not even a marine radio out there. It's not good, should anything happen to you or your wife."

Jim made no attempt to encourage her. "We've got everything we need on the island."

"Well, no matter. I've got an old marine radio that we don't use, and I monitor our base station for distress. You could always get someone on Channel 16. It would at least be some communication to let us know you're okay."

"Sure. I suppose we can pick it up on our return." He turned to the mechanic. "So, could we rent a boat for a few days so that you can get ours into the shop?"

"No problem. I have an older sixteen-foot inboard. Runs well, has a top. You mentioned going to Winnipeg. Are you still going today?"

Jim told him we would be back well before dark. We did not want to delay our trip with colder weather coming in.

We were given the rental boat keys as we left. The couple appeared to be pretty nice people with a genuine concern for our welfare, and perhaps not just our pocketbook. I realized the marine phone was a good idea, especially in light of what just happened, but I knew Jim would have resistance to the possibility of our whereabouts or our well-being being monitored.

We had reviewed weather conditions of the area. It appeared that winter started in this part of northwestern Ontario no later than October 31ˢᵗ, when trick-or-treaters were faced with the first cold blast of snow from the Arctic. December through to February were the coldest months, with nighttime temperatures between -6°F and -36°F or colder. Daytime temperatures could hover at -6°F for weeks. Winter was not over at the end of February. It just meant that each month until near the end of May got warmer, bit by bit. Ice-out could be anywhere from the end of April to mid-May.

I reviewed the list as Jim drove. Cases of various pasta, canned vegetables, rice, paper products. And all of it into our half-ton truck, into a boat, and onto the island. I was already tired.

CHAPTER 6

THE EARLY DAYS

It was astonishing how those fall days slipped by on our Lake of the Woods island when we first arrived. Exerted muscles with aches and pains blended into the late fall days so that the passing of time had no meaning. The days of the week were marked off on the calendar as a reminder of our schedule, of projects that needed completion if we were to survive the winter. Each completion was greeted with another beginning.

Jim had lost almost twenty pounds since we arrived and a physical regime that pushed his muscles to their limit. Just months before, he had experienced the anger and loss of control that comes with battling bureaucrats, frustration with his inability to move his public company forward with a Board of Directors made up largely of lawyers.

What he had not realized at the time is how unbalanced his life had become. He had abandoned his own physical being. He had relied almost solely on the strength of mind. Added stress. Added pounds. His blood pressure skyrocketed. Shockingly, finding out that he had Type II diabetes.

With a new beginning and twenty pounds already shed, the blood pressure went back to normal and there was no sign of diabetes. Something else happened as well. I could see his self-awareness returning. There was something magically happening, a connection between mind and body. He had expressed it to me in terms of his sports training. He described it as an intimate awareness of one's body, acuteness to every sensation and ultimately conscious mastery of this extremely powerful body mass. I could not relate because of my limited experience with sports. I was envious of that mind and body connection, a mastery of the physical self, knowing your capacity. I had a difficult time unifying my mind and emotions, let alone harmony of mind and body.

There were fewer and fewer boats on the lake as October slipped by, and that is why I was surprised to see the twenty-six-foot Sea Ray tuck itself neatly beside our boathouse. Jim was applying the last strip of rolled roofing over the strapped polystyrene insulation on the backside of the cabin roof.

"Jim, we have company."

"I'm not getting off the roof just to chat," he shouted down.

"I'll see who it is." Sekima, our malamute bounded ahead of me.

I met him as he was crossing the ramp out of the boathouse. About my age, a tall, large-framed man with an unkempt blonde beard and full head of wispy hair, large dark sunglasses. He extended his hand. "Paul. Paul Warner. Just passing through and wanted to know if you folks needed anything."

"Connie." My hand was small in his grip. "Come on up to the cabin." I led him to the rear where Jim was just getting off the ladder.

"Hi. I'm Jim." This was the first guy Jim had met since we'd arrived that was remotely close to his size. They stood head-to-head.

"Name's Paul. You're not from these parts." It was a statement, not a question. "I see you have a bit of a job ahead of you. Some people in town say you're staying the winter." He played with Sekima as he spoke. "You're a happy one, aren't you?" he extended his elbow to avoid getting jumped on.

"Sekima! Down! I'm originally from Chicago and Connie is from the Ottawa area, near Algonquin Park."

Paul told us he'd lived here most of his life. He ran a barge and worked on the lake mostly.

"Would you deliver wood?" It was our biggest challenge. We had not secured a contract for wood, and although there was some deadfall on the island, we would need more. We wanted to keep the hardwood, all white birch, on our island.

Paul said he could deliver it with his barge. "I'd have to rent a Bobcat to unload." He pivoted around still talking as we walked. "You would want the wood as close as you can to the back door. I don't see any road." He appeared to be including us in a discussion he was having with himself.

I winced at the mention of a road. That meant clearing trees. I liked the landscape just as it was.

Paul stuck his gloveless hands into his oil-stained canvas coat and headed down a path that led to a deck on the lake. We followed closely behind. It was about a hundred yards from the boathouse.

"Oh, not good." He shook his head slightly from side to side. "Look, right there." He pointed. "See that nicely pointed rock Jim? It's the kind that the barge can get hung up on until the lake rises. No sirree, don't want to get near that one. Pretty shallow here too."

We hadn't considered it before. It was something we knew needed to be done, but we didn't know how major deliveries were made.

Paul turned to the small deck that served as our favorite spot to watch the sun rise and set. "It looks like I could bring it in right here. See how the rock goes straight down. Drops off good. I could lower the ramp right here on this big old piece of granite."

The price was going to be somewhere around eighty dollars a cord, then there was barge time, Bobcat rental, and Paul. By the time all was said and done, it looked close to $2,000 to stay warm. There was no definite date on delivery, just as soon as he could. It would have to be before he started hunting.

"Some people have already said you're a bit crazy staying out here this winter. You'd likely not want them as friends anyways." It seemed a strange offering on his part and piqued our interest—well, at least mine. We had not met anyone but the marina folk. I wondered if it was them.

"We met Joe and Nora from the marina. They insisted we bring their portable marine radio out here. It's not our style to be phoning in regularly." Jim still thought it was a mistake.

"Stopped that during high school, I imagine," Paul chuckled. "Look if there's anything I can help you with around the place, I got the wherewithal."

With no particular salesmanship, he explained that besides barging he built new cabins, boathouses, set cribs, and docks.

"You don't happen to know anything about old Servel fridges, do you?" Jim was talking about our propane refrigerator that had come with the cabin. It seemed to work fine for a while, and then would randomly stop working. Jim had a lot of experience with propane, but the Servel was a mystery.

"What seems to be the trouble? They usually work or they don't work."

"I know there's not much that can go wrong with them," Jim said. "I used to work with Canadian Western Natural Gas, so know a fair bit. The trouble is the pilot light. It won't stay on. I know there's propane coming through. I've also cleaned it."

"I know a guy that works on them. Easy enough for me to bring him out one of these days. If there's anyone that can fix one of those Servels, it's him. What about propane bottle refills? I guess you're going to have an ice road plowed?"

It was a relief to connect with someone that knew people in the service industry, and if we got far enough along, Paul just might be the guy to do a few of the bigger projects we anticipated. The ice road was not our priority, not this year. There just was not enough money, and we were not planning on going anywhere.

Jim said, "We weren't intending on it. We bought enough food staples to do us until spring."

"It's all dry and canned goods. Perhaps not a lot of variety, but everything will be from scratch," I added.

Paul cautioned us. He didn't know how much propane we would use, but from experience with ice roads, we would not be able to build one in the middle of winter.

"You do that too, eh?" I couldn't help my curiosity.

"Sure do. Come to think of it, there's a guy that might be needing some work done this winter, just to the west of you. I could likely make a pass this way."

It sounded pretty good to me, but I could tell Jim wanted to stay focused on our priorities.

"No decisions need to be made now," Paul said. "I still have to firm up a few things with this guy anyways."

We took no time in concluding after that. The first shadows of dusk were evident, and there were still tools to get off the roof. Paul sped away in the Sea Ray. We were not totally alone on the lake.

CHAPTER 7

NOWHERE TO HIDE

Winter was knocking at our door. The log cabin had been built in 1946. Its original honey logs in the interior stained a dirty ugly red on the exterior. The logs were tight, a chinking like steel wool between them. We had purchased polystyrene foam panels to put over the exterior walls and roof.

Where possible, we dug around the perimeter of the cabin so that the panels would go below the first log row. The cabin sat on concrete pads and existing granite. We wanted to prevent winter air flow underneath it. We had taken a candle around the interior and found numerous spots in the floor that were allowing air to enter. Every flickering flame meant a potential of a few degrees of warmth slipping away, or, more likely, a frigid breeze slipping in.

When we finished, the dirty red exterior was white with polystyrene and vertical and horizontal strapping from an old, smaller boathouse we had dismantled. The roof had taken the longest, six inches of foam, sheathing, and rolled roofing. As with most trapper log cabins, ours sat low in profile, with doors a six-foot man had to duck to get through.

We were near enough to all we would be able to accomplish before winter. There was frost most mornings and weather would change quickly with no warning. We had a heightened awareness, an eagerness to embrace the unknown. We had prepared as much as we could. Now, the only thing we could do was give way to nature and its primal cycles, its creatures all knowing. Squirrels were busy storing pine cones; beavers were appearing more regularly, swimming our shoreline looking for potential winter food; deer had already masked themselves with their muted grey-brown coats. Sekima had grown a luxurious double coat, looking more like his wolf ancestors than ever. He was wolf-grey with brown, an imposing big face, and a lion mane that extended around his shoulders.

We had found that our collapsible water line was going to work, at least at the temperatures we were now experiencing. The lake was no longer sapphire blue but a steel grey, reflecting the overcast October sky. Our weekly showers were accompanied by a VCR movie night, popcorn, and Pepsi. The ritual was reserved for once a week primarily to conserve gasoline. A small portable Coleman gas generator had been left by the previous owners. We had filled several gas cans, and, along with everything else, it had to make it through the winter. The gas generator was compact and light enough to store inside the cabin to keep it warm for easy starting. While its capacity was limited, it was big enough to pump the water and run the television with an old VCR machine. The box of VCR tapes was a culmination of years of collecting and always seemed a luxury after a week of lantern reading.

Workload had decreased, and finally we were able to fish from the shoreline. The north shore was sixty feet deep, the south shore over two hundred feet. We cast from the shore for northern pike. They were the big boys that dominated the deeps, with the exception of the lake trout that would not come up to our casting lures. The northern ranged from thirty-eight to forty-three inches in length, with reptilian heads, widespread mouths, and extensive razor teeth. They were great eating fish—large steaks and solid fillets. It would take sometimes up to an hour to bring one in, a commitment to wait and tire it out. Acting too soon, the powerful fish would break the line and head for the deep. We did not have faith in our little boat for long distances. The shallower walleye waters were too far. The boat sat bow out safely in our boathouse.

Our preparedness for winter had taken an incredible amount of focus and energy. We realized that if we failed there was no one to blame but ourselves, and that failing would be giving up on our dream. We had no Plan B. We were on a shipwrecked island. There was no time to be fearful, no time to fret over decisions. We had already made them, and our lives were set in motion.

I cannot recall now what our discussion was that led to my need to escape one night. For the most part I had let Jim take the lead. I may have had a construction company, but I had knowledgeable people to do the work. Now, I was the lightweight laborer. There cannot be two bosses. So, over dinner, we disagreed about something. It could have been about next steps. I felt strongly. So did he. I did not expect it. He had always been intense. It was one of the things that I loved about him. His passion was obvious. He was a serious guy, confident and handsome, with a powerful jaw and flashing light blue eyes. One minute we were sitting there debating about a next step, and then we were arguing. It was the first time I had ever felt threatened by him.

He raised his voice. I could feel his intensity. His eyes penetrated through me with command. I felt fear hit me like a raging storm, and I wanted to take my hands and put them over my ears, but I was incapable of moving. *No, no, no.* I could hear my internal voice. *Run, run, run,* it said. The outhouse was always a good reason to have to go outside, and somehow, I got my body to move. He did not know. He did not suspect. I was out the door. I was out the door with nowhere to go on an isolated island.

I needed to hide. The sun had gone down, and I could not see well. There was a deathly silence; everything was shut off but my mind. I made my way down to the boathouse. There it was, the un-sunk boat, the same red and white plastic seats, a front canvas cover over the bow that was big enough for me. My hiding spot. I could barely make it under the tonneau cover.

I shivered in the cold. I had no way of escaping. Emotions, void of reason, panic, blackness—a flight response. I curled in fetal position. I did not hear the wind or the waves. I heard only my fearful despair, crawling tentacles in my brain, collecting haunting terror stories. They gathered together forming a continuous loop, faster and faster, racing towards the finish line. I had nowhere to run.

Time rescued me. I struggled to regain control of runaway thoughts. Seconds, counting heartbeats. Minutes passing, draining the fear away. Sifting through our conversation looking for the threat that had driven me to run. There had been no hateful berating, no belittling or personal verbal attack, no raised hand or pounding of fist on the table.

In a flash of memory, it came back to me. The fear, the anticipation of terrible fighting, my father slamming his fist on the table, loud, angry voices penetrating the walls. We were told to go hide in our rooms by our mother, who trembled in fear and anger. Her husband was late, which meant he was drinking. By the time he made it home, she would have exhausted her worry, leaving her with loathsome rage. The voices were so loud, so hateful. There was nowhere to run, no way for me to get away. Was my present fear justified?

I am not sure how long I was there. I am not sure how long I waited. I heard Jim calling my name.

"Connie, if you are in here, please come out." His voice was soft and gentle.

"I'm here." I did not move.

"You need to know, I would never, ever, hurt you."

It was what I needed to hear. Those simple words. There had been no personal attack in his raised voice, no bitterness in our disagreement. But now there was an understanding of my basic truth: I was afraid of being hurt. I had always been able to run before. My body trembled and slow, sad tears dripped painful rivulets of memory.

It was not just the old memories of my parents fighting. It started there, but it went from that small child and her interpretation of danger to a real predator. I remember the simple dress I wore. It was so pretty. It had a white top with elastic around the short sleeves and frock line, and the waistline. The white top had a little bow at the neckline. The bottom was a mosaic of green, white, and yellow on a dark brown backdrop. I do not remember if it was printed with leaves or a pattern of the time. I think the latter. I ran. I ran hard and fast for my life. And then again, I ran. I wore an old shirt, a hand-me-down from my brother. It was so worn that I could see my training bras through it. It was long, with full sleeves that I had to roll up. I loved that shirt. But my uncle sat me on his knee and felt my small breasts, and asked me if I liked it. I did not. And I ran.

The scars are permanent, indelibly stamped like a tattoo, fading and blurring over time. The men I ran from, I do not know how many. They were discarded for reasons they did not know. The bad dudes, the wimpy, overly kind, the ex that would never know. And even now I thought I should run. I was trained to run. But I could not. There was nowhere to go. The scars would always be there, but I was suddenly glad there was nowhere to go. It was time to just wait. It was time to face the demons.

Had I been able to run, I would never have found out. I would never have been found.

CHAPTER 8

CAUTION IN THE WIND

Paul was true to his word. Less than a week later, on a windy October 30th, we made our way down by the shoreline to watch the slow-moving barge. It was clearly over two miles away and although we had only seen a few lake barges, we were certain there were no boats that would be visible at that distance. Save for a couple of hunters, we had not seen any boats for quite some time.

I was exuberant, waving my hands in the air and doing a gleeful dance. I enjoyed this lifestyle, where I could dance with nature every day. The silence but for waves and wind, the resilient pines swaying, the bruised sunsets and blackened starry nights. I could dance. I could sway slowly to the blues in the woeful calls of the loon. I could dance to folk songs, to rock and roll, to country tunes as the lake rippled lightly and churned with froth, as the winds sent poplar leaves musically fluttering and branches angrily snapping.

The barge was twenty feet wide by eighty feet long, eighty ton in total, and with fifteen cord of birch logs, it was an imposing sight coming to shore. Paul had chosen the spot we discussed, next to our small flat deck, our east and west view of the lake. The large granite outcropping allowed him to lower his ramp on solid rock where the water was deep. The steel made a heavy grinding noise as it rubbed the granite shoreline. Paul exited the tug swiftly. With a quick "Hi, folks," he sprang from the barge, rope in hand and ran nimbly down the shoreline until he found a suitable tree to tie off on. Having done this, multiple ropes on both sides to his satisfaction, he casually walked over, those large dark sunglasses always shading his eyes and his thoughts. "Well Jim, what do you think? Enough wood for winter?" he asked in a serious tone.

"Enough to keep us warm and me busy."

It was our best guess, and we hoped it was enough for winter.

"This is heavenly. Absolutely, fantastic." I held onto Sekima, knowing he was about to body slam Paul. I'm sure my smile sent rays of appreciation.

Paul chuckled. "I'll be leaving the barge and tug here overnight and taking the Sea Ray home. It's going to take me a few hours to get the logs off and there's no use starting now."

"That big rig will be okay for the night in these winds?" I asked tentatively.

"I assure you. It will. I tied it off and that spot can't get any more wave to it because of that island north of you. No winds coming from the east or west tonight. You'll be checking those winds every day, living out here."

Jim tried to get my attention with the look. It was a look of reassurance that Paul knew what he was doing.

"A coffee or something?" I asked. "Jim will probably share his blueberry pie."

"Finest crust anywhere," Jim offered.

"Not for me, but maybe you have a pint of something before I take off." Paul slapped his stomach as though the pie would be too many calories.

Three pints later, Paul was at liberty to tell us about how he came to be on the lake.

"My grandfather, he got his hands on a whole bunch of these islands and a good chunk of land down Morrison way. He started out as a commercial fisherman, back in the day when this lake was the biggest supplier of caviar to the world."

The firebox of the small cast iron cookstove, fondly called the PIG because it devoured wood so quickly, crackled as he spoke.

"So, sturgeon, eh?" I couldn't help but get the odd "eh" into my conversation to indicate I wanted to hear more.

"They pulled caviar out of here until the later 1800s, about the same time they cut the white pine off the islands to build Chicago."

Jim had done his own research about the lake and knew Paul's story to be true. Still, it did not appear that Paul was successor to a big estate.

"We had this pet black bear. I recall sleeping on the porch with this damn thing cuddling around me. It was the funniest thing." He stroked his blond beard as he spoke. Sunglasses finally dismissed; his blue eyes were laughing.

"What about now, Paul? Did your grandfather sell off all his land?" I asked.

"Nah. Didn't get to sell anything but the homestead in Morrison. Gambled the rest. Lost it all in a poker game."

"Oh, you're kidding. What a tragedy." I felt bad for him.

Paul tipped the remains of his beer as though ending the chapter.

"Another?" I asked, pointing at the empty.

Jim had never been fond of heavy drinking. It did not fit with his football days or his philosophy on life. I knew I should not be encouraging Paul, but it was so nice to have company, and his story was fascinating. He was a big enough guy, and there did not seem to be any visible signs of intoxication.

He explained that he'd best be getting home. The dogs had to get fed and his own fire was likely going out by now. His mood turned serious and somber. "You seem like nice folks. And I just want to warn you—you'll find out quickly who your friends are in these parts."

"What do you mean?" Jim asked.

"It's better you don't say too much. Just sit back and watch. You know what I mean?"

"I don't get it," I persisted.

"Just watch for the signs. I'm not going to say any more than that. You'll need to find out for yourselves." Paul dismissed me.

I was baffled by his comments. Jim did not get it either. It was a way of communicating for Paul. Some people just preferred to set up a trail to follow rather than telling it straight. Jim saw it as a sign of manipulation, but shrugged it off. Nice enough guy, and our wood was almost on the island.

Just like he said he would, Paul did arrive the next morning and before we could get our coats on, we heard the rumble of the small skid steer being started up. Given that we had not discussed where to put the logs, or even where he was going to make a road to bring them up on, we hurried out. We both appreciated every tree on the island and we were unsure that Paul felt the same way.

It had snowed overnight, but it was melting with the earth's warmth. The witches snow of Halloween lay heavy like a wet sock on the ground.

"Hey-yoah." He met us on the path with his usual greeting. "I'm thinking you'll probably want to come up just over there a bit. It's all small scrub brush. No big trees need to come out."

I was relieved that he was thinking that way. We discussed the various advantages of where to place the logs near the house and then got out of his way.

By midday, Paul had completed hauling the large birch logs, some of them over twelve inches in diameter, onto the island. The side of the hill was stripped, the ground peeled back exposing all the clay that a good rock island could muster. Paul had cut a swath ten feet wide from the deck to the top of the hill. At the top, he had piled the birch logs over twelve feet high. He had neutered an area bigger than the house, tank tracks in some places deeper than any man's boot. There was plain old gumbo everywhere that immediately stuck to our boots like honey to a spoon. Many of the logs looked like they had been dipped in it, then rolled in sand like a corndog.

There was not anything to be done about it, and likely nothing Paul could have done about it either. One thing was certain: we would be stuck with clay in our back yard for years to come. Paul was like that. He would get the job done. The outcome was not always predictable. It took us time, but we learned. He would always choose brute force over finesse. He was constantly exposing himself and anyone around him to the challenges of the land and lake, likely more than anyone wanted.

CHAPTER 9

LOST

We had barely taken a break since we moved to the island. There was an endless stream of things to do before winter set in. Most of my assistance was limited to taking instructions from Jim. Hold that board. Bring him this or that. There was a lot of taking things apart before putting things together.

A small abandoned boathouse was the perfect source for boards, spikes, and nails. At times it seemed impossible to imagine why we would physically dismantle a building, and how it would make a difference. But at the end of each day, we sat at the small pine table, coal oil lantern flickering shadows on our meal, feeling confident that we were stepping in time with the rhythm of nature.

By the second week of November, we were ready for a bit of a break and hopefully get some deer meat for winter. An island just west of us seemed a good choice, close enough for our little red boat. I would walk the length of the island at a steady pace, hopefully moving any deer towards Jim where he would take a stand at the end. We left Sekima in the cabin, believing he was a bit young to take out on a hunt.

As soon as I was dropped off, I knew I was confronting big physical challenges. The bush already had snow up to my knees in places where it had drifted between trees. I'd had plenty of physical exercise in the last few months, but nothing that came close to this.

I swore silently as I fought each step to make forward progress. Every few steps I met with another fallen spruce. It was as though the trees had been thrown from a wooden match box, landing askew. Many fallen trees were higher than my waist so that I had to belly over them, grappling to hold onto my 32 Winchester rifle. It was deadfall as far as I could see. Between the toppled giants, the snow was deeply drifted.

By the time I reached a clear passage, where the trees were less dense, a half hour had already passed, about the time that we had anticipated that I would come out. I was certain that Jim would already be wondering what was taking me so long. I found a point high up on a ridge looking out over a very large bay below. I winced at what I saw. The bay stretched a quarter mile across. I would have to go a longer distance, around it, from the very top of the island. I could also go below, skirt the dense underbrush of the shoreline of the bay itself, if I continued in the same direction. If I stayed above it, I would have to go deeper into the woods, but it was better than the tangled mass below. My compass did not mean much until I could take southerly bearings after I was deep in the forest.

The interior woods had become less treacherous, yet twenty minutes seemed an eternity. It was time once again to make my way to the edge of the ridge and pinpoint where I was on the map I carried. Jim had coached me that it was impossible to get lost on an island. All I had to do was come out to water and look where I was. Too much time had passed and I still had not found a reference point. I climbed to a high enough point to see out across an expanse of water. None of what I saw confirmed anything. The more I looked at the islands beyond and the map in my hands, the more anxiety I felt. It was like trying to finish a puzzle and finding that the last piece did not fit. I marked off two or three islands that seemed to match, but then where there was supposed to be another, there was not. It meant I was wrong. I did not know where I was. I was lost.

How many times had I felt this way in my life? I could not find that reference point. A point of beginning, no point where I could just take the time to get my bearings. And the harder I tried, the more confused I felt. It seemed that all that I knew meant little. As I looked for something tangible, the disorientation took hold. I became anxious because I really knew nothing at all that applied. I tried so hard to find something that made any sense of it all.

Having run out of time and willingness to go on, I made way down the steep elevation. Perhaps if I got a glimpse of the shoreline, I would be able to recognize something, otherwise I would set in motion my rescue. From above, natural underbrush mixed with heavy spruce made it impossible for me to see shore. The closer I got to the water's edge, the heavier the underbrush became. The dense deadfall was now replaced with a swath of thicket swiping at my face. It reeled me back as my gun harness or coat would catch on the layer of brittle and jagged shrubs. Finally, returning to the water's edge, I studied the contours of my surroundings. It was yet another bay, indistinguishable from the last.

The island was well over a hundred acres and none of it symmetrical. There were several bays on this easterly shore, indentations that looked like someone had doodled the shoreline in place. It was just a matter of identifying which one of those I was in. The more I looked, the more disoriented I became. *It could not be. Yes, it could. Not possible.* Self-doubt clouded my judgment, and finally I gave in to uncertainty.

I folded up the map and jammed it into my backpack. I took out a piece of Hungarian sausage and a coffee thermos. I had run out of options. I was lost. It was clear that for all my desire to be one with nature, I was an absolute failure at simple directional coordinates of a compass in the woods. I would wait.

I threw off my soggy gloves and pumped a shell into the chamber. *Bang . . . Bang . . . Bang . . .* the signal for lost. I took a bit of the spicy sausage and sipped bitter coffee. I needed to build a fire that would help Jim locate me.

My decision to stop moving gave me a sense of comfort, removing the anxiety that I felt each time I tried to determine where I was. For the time being, I was not worried. Jim would be my hero. I had never been in Girl Scouts, but living on the island with only wood as a source of heat made me skilled at starting fires. I selected pinecones, small twigs, and the bigger variety. I used No Name paper towels from lunch as the starter. The paper burnt well, but after that—nothing, not even an ember. It was obvious, I had not taken this seriously enough.

I went on a wider search. I gathered bigger, fluffier pinecones, the tiniest of twigs, and tufts of brown grass that I uncovered under the snow. I changed my location so that the fire would be out of the wind, hidden behind a granite bolder. Five matches were struck before I got a flame from the grass. It was definitely worse than the paper towel. Nature's offering was soggy wet.

Returning once more to the remains in my backpack, I decided on the cardboard box from my gun shells. I placed it in the center of a neat pile of cones, grass and twigs, teepee style. It was not exactly the same as nice dry kindling with a dash of kerosene, but it had the makings. If this was to be my last attempt, then I was prepared to risk it all, light the whole matchbook at once. *Poof!* Lovely yellow flame engulfed my triangle. It peaked and shed warmth, then slowly dwindled to nothing, leaving me furiously blowing on the ends of twigs that had a slight glow.

I had stopped moving. I had stopped with absolute abandon. I gave in to the realization that I knew nothing at all. I had thrown away my final resources. I had risked it all, perhaps too quickly It was not arrogance, but it certainly was an abandonment of myself.

Reality struck. It was two hours past the time when we were to meet. A northerly wind was driving into my face across the bay turning perspiration to chilly icicles sliding down my torso. The temperature was dropping quickly. I had devoured my food, and I was completely out of fire starter. I slipped further into fear and doubt for the tenth time today.

I believed that Jim would have known I was lost some time ago. It should have taken minutes for him to drive the boat around the island to find me. Even without a fire, my brilliant orange hunting clothes could not be missed. But I hadn't heard the familiar boat motor. *Had he broken down? Worse yet, had he hurt himself?*

I understood now that I had made a fatal mistake. I had rationalized my way out of being afraid, to a state of carelessness. When I finally made it down to the shoreline, I decided someone was going to save me. I gave up. Someone outside of me was my savior. I had placed myself in harm's way. I should not have waited. Deciding to wait to be rescued could be a disastrous mistake. *Why was I waiting for someone else to save me? Why had I given up on myself so quickly, so many times in my life?*

I had let my guard down. I had acted like it did not really matter. Jim would find me regardless. How could he miss me? The making of a fire was really just pretend. Like pretending you are going to go on a diet, but only lasting a day. Like pretending you will quit smoking when you have finished the pack of cigarettes that you just bought. How many times had I let that happen in my life, pretending that something was important, but really quitting before I even began? How many times had I abandoned myself by waiting for someone else to do it for me?

Boom! Boom! Boom! I pumped three more shells into the air in desperation. *Why hasn't Jim found me?*

Another thirty minutes passed as I sat frozen in panic. I could not try to locate Jim at this point. The shoreline was impassable, too steep with jagged rock, and too dense with bush where it sloped gently to the water. It meant I would have to climb up to the top again, and if he did come along, he would not see me. *I'm too tired to climb that ravine again. I can't just sit here and wait. Is there anything else that will light a fire? Stop it! Stop this panic!*

Suddenly, a familiar voice came drifting down from above, "Connie."

"I'm here. Here!" I yelled. "Jim, where are you?" I frantically searched the ledges above. Covered with saw-toothed rock, scattered deadfall, brush and majestic evergreen, the escarpment appeared a woven mesh. My eyesight was unable to penetrate it.

"Jim!" I screamed. I could hear the shriek of my own voice blown away in the wind.

Finally, Jim's voice was closer now. "Connie, I'm up here."

The brilliant orange in his jacket appeared above me. My eyes filled up with tears.

"Make your way up," he yelled.

"Where's the boat?"

"It's on the other side of the island," he said, his voice barely audible in the wind.

Branches slapped my face as I made my way once again to the top of the island. I was oblivious of the path I chose. I didn't care. The quicker I got to Jim the better. By the time I reached him, my hair and clothing were full of twigs and branches. I hugged him and clung tightly to that familiar strength.

"I couldn't find you with the boat," he said. He eased me away, setting our course. "Follow me."

"How far?" I asked. I was already sweating and tired from my climb up the ravine.

"The boat is on the other side. Not more than a half hour walk. We should get going. It's late." He had already started off ahead.

After a half hour, I felt my enthusiasm and physical strength evaporate simultaneously. The snow was over a foot deep in places, heavy and thick; it was like wading through one of those DQ or

Sonic ice cream mixes. I had tried to imagine them as puffy cumulous clouds, but the snow's resistance was real.

"I have to stop. How much further?"

"Not far," he said. "We'll rest here for a bit."

Jim had relieved me of weight, taken my gun and my pack. Bright crystals of light danced on the snow cover. Droplets of ice clung to the tips of branches already too late in the day to be released by the sun. There was so much beauty in nature, even in my fatigue.

Jim was waiting patiently. Finally, I struggled to lift my weight from the log I had been resting on. Within minutes, I was once again lagging.

"Slow down. I'm tired," I cried out. I stumbled over fallen branches. My steps were labored. I was stopping more frequently now. I took relief by flopping in the snow for a brief minute. The snow was like a pillow, and felt refreshing against my face, an immediate icepack. I dragged myself up, on the move again, letting Jim get further and further from reach.

"Jim! Jim!" I screamed.

"Are you okay?" he yelled from a distance.

I felt shaken that I was this far behind, fearing that I would lose sight of his tracks. The panic of being lost earlier played on my mind. The bush was dense, woven like a catcher's mitt. Jim was not easily lost in the entanglement of the deep northern woods. But I was losing track of him. The stillness I had often cherished in the Canadian Shield was now a large silent abyss ready to swallow me.

I didn't answer Jim. *I just don't think I can make it. I'm not even sure that I care.* Again, I was looking for a savior. Tears stung. I was exhausted and humiliated that I could not keep up. I realized now that Jim was purposely putting distance between us to keep me going. It was a survival trick that he had told me about.

I'm just going to stay here for a while. Everything was still, quiet, peaceful. *I could sleep right here, wait until I get my strength back.*

If I could just rest, I would be refreshed in a while. Sleep for a while. Somewhere in the void, I sensed another part of me, an instinct to survive taking control. *Get up! Fight!*

I shook myself out of my slumber. I reached for a branch to help me get up. It cracked and broke, sending me flying backwards onto the base of a gnarled jack pine. Struggling to my feet, I pushed myself forward, one step at a time, following the trail of footsteps in the snow. I detached from the pain and weariness, knowing that I must follow. It was up to me. I would follow.

At dusk we arrived back at the boat. The sixteen-foot aluminum, scarred by the use of twenty years, was a heavenly sight. We pushed off from shore with a blow of northwest wind that was roughly fifteen knots. Shadows of dusk reached over us, changing the color of the lake to an ominous black.

One hundred yards out, the motor sputtered and died. Jim turned the key. The starter engaged, turning the motor over and over.

"What's going on?"

"I don't know." He slipped to the back of the boat, checking the rubber gas tank connections, and tried again. It sounded tired.

I could not believe this was happening. I had heard so often of things turning bad in nature, one thing leading to another. Murphy's Law, when anything that can go wrong, will go wrong. I sat in silence. I was of no use to Jim. His jaw was set, his face rigid and tense. I knew him well enough to keep quiet and let him think. I watched him pump the gas, clean away deposits of caked snow and ice from wires, and all the time our position worsened. The northerly wind howled, blowing the boat opposite of the path that led home, driving us south. The waves were vicious, nearing two feet, shooting the little boat like a deflating helium balloon towards open and bigger waters. If we got propelled into the big water, we would have no refuge.

"Can't we paddle back to shore?" I yelled above the waves.

"What's that going to do."

"We're drifting pretty fast, Jim."

He glanced sideways and ignored my comment.

"Here. You keep pushing on this ball as hard as you can," he instructed. "I don't think it's getting gas."

Clunk . . . .clunk . . . clunk . . . grind. I careened sideways, losing my hold on the gas line. The boat shuddered and spun like a top. It pivoted, holding its breath for a moment, and fell on its side, tipping over, depositing me on the floor of the hull.

"We hit something!" I screamed.

"We're on a reef," he yelled above the wind.

"Did we wreck anything?"

"I don't think so."

The reef suddenly stopped us from getting swept further down the lake. A sudden gift amidst our disastrous day. The last rays of sunlight had disappeared and darkness set in. It was a cold, threatening November night.

"Jim, I think we should call it quits," I pleaded.

"And do what?" he said angrily.

"The island is not far. We could paddle and set up camp for the night."

"We could never paddle this thing with the wind. If we could make it, we would be up all night in this weather. They've predicted -3F tonight."

"The battery is going to run down."

He had turned away from me and now flicked a sideways glance. "It won't be any better in the morning."

I gave the gas line another fierce squeeze. "The motor might be too cold. We could wait until it warms up tomorrow afternoon."

Jim looked grim. "That could be spring in Canada."

"You don't even know what's wrong with it." I was tired,

frustrated, and very frightened. "It's dark. I can hardly see shore. I think we should make camp before we can't see anything."

"We're going to keep trying this motor until the battery is dead."

The tone of his voice told me his decision was final. So often, we would banter back and forth, until someone finally gave in, or changed their mind. In this instance, I knew his word was not only final, but his experience was far superior to my own.

"Is there any way we can manually start it?"

"Maybe. It's just not getting gas. Or there's water in the gas."

I squatted low in the back of the boat, pulling my toque down over my eyebrows, submissively, like a sorry pup. I knew he had the experience and stamina. I continued to squeeze the primer ball. My hands and wrists ached from effort, until I finally lost consciousness of time. I prayed to God, the universe, and Mother Nature to take us home safely.

Suddenly, the motor caught, sputtered and died, caught again. I felt a wave of gratitude, tingling with jubilation. We were in gear and slowly moving forward off the reef. I waited in anticipation for Jim to give the boat full throttle and speed us home. We were barely making any headway against the wind.

"What's happening?" I shouted.

"This is it. It won't go any faster."

I watched him frozen to the steering wheel, one hand still holding in the choke. He had long since abandoned his gloves. His jaw was clenched, lips drawn back with tell-tale lines of pain outlining his mouth.

I sat silently trying to will us home. The final rays of dusk had disappeared. The clear cold sky and moon shed light on shorelines. I imagined the nocturnal animals starting to stir. We passed cabins that had already been deserted for winter, and then the final turn to the east through a channel that gave us relief from the wind.

We finally arrived at our boathouse. Exhaustion flooded my

body. My mind had been trapped in another dimension, a void to shut out the cold and fatigue. We left the boat and arrived at the cabin door. Jim moved towards me, held me in his arms for a moment. He cupped my face with cold hands. In a whispering, deep voice, he spoke. "We're home, safe."

Inside with a fire roaring, we drank a double Scotch. There were lessons to be remembered. With the additional time taken to maneuver through the deadfall, I had not realized that I did not make it more than a quarter mile down the shoreline. In turn, when Jim realized something was amiss, he had used the boat to search the shoreline for me. Given my proximity to the starting point, he did not look in that first bay. He did not hear the first set of shots over the boat engine. Without finding me on the shoreline, he determined that I must be hurt somewhere in the interior of the island. He started where he thought he had the best chance of finding me. There were always calculated risks that we took, but miscalculation was always in the equation, an unforgiving unknown. Sometimes lost, sometimes found.

CHAPTER 10

GIFTS OF NATURE

Paul's familiar Sea Ray, the Promiscuous Queen, pulled up at the boathouse one morning just after a light snowfall. We watched through our frosted windows as he faked a dodge with Sekima and made his way to the back door, dressed in bright orange hunting garb.

"Come on in." I answered the rapid *tap, tap,* of his knock.

He opened the door and was met by a large brown blanket of faux beaver that prevented the cold from seeping through cracks between the wooden door and its jamb. He had to move it off to the side and duck to get under it.

"Hey! I thought that was some beaver pelt you had hanging." He chuckled.

"It's a fake. We found it upstairs in the attic."

"Look, I picked up some people this morning. We're going to chase a few islands for deer. Thought you might want to come?" he asked.

"Jim?" I turned questioningly.

We had been discussing our possibilities of being successful hunting these big islands with just the two of us. This was a good opportunity to gain some knowledge of islands we knew little about.

"Sure. I have to get my gear on but it will only take a few minutes. What about you, Connie?"

"If there's room?"

Paul reassured us that the islands were big. It would give four to push and three to shoot.

"This gear is hotter than hell, so I'll go outside and wait for you in the boat." His big felt insulated rubber boots left puddles of melting snow in the kitchen doorway.

They were waiting for us in the Sea Ray. The introductions were brief as Paul thrust the powerful engine into reverse. "Jim, Connie, this is Norm, Wacko, Dale, and Thunder." He started with the white guy, who smiled and nodded, followed by three Indigenous men who followed suit.

There were no available seats in the Sea Ray's hull so I made myself as comfortable as I could between Jim and Paul, sitting on a life jacket, back up against the small cabin door that would lead to below deck bunks.

I could not help but take in Wacko's features. With a name like Wacko, I figured there must be something a bit strange about this dude. Wacko had sunglasses like Paul's—big, black wrap-arounds that shielded his eyes and thoughts. Hunter-orange toque framed a large, round face. Slightly flattened nose tilted sideways from the bridge to the nostril, showing signs of having been broken. Full lips with large stained teeth that glistened against his burnt-umber-colored skin when he smiled. A deep scar extended from his chin and disappeared under his collar. He was a tad scary looking.

He popped open his backpack, pulled out an oversized beer can and plucked the tab of a sixteen ouncer. I was sure he was looking right at me when he lifted the can, held it in the air for a moment, and said, "Breakfast."

I smiled. I had worn my fluorescent orange lipstick to match my vest and hat. I did it jokingly, insisting to Jim that I never knew who

I might meet in the bush. I was sure Wacko thought I was a city slicker. The testosterone around me was a bit unnerving. I did not want to be placed on a deer stand. There would be so much pressure for me to shoot a deer. I might miss. But if I opted to chase and get lost again, I would simply die of embarrassment.

"Jim. I think I'd prefer to chase than sit."

"You brought your compass?" he asked.

"That doesn't mean I can't get turned around." I voiced my anxiety.

"What island are we doing first, Paul?" Jim inquired.

"Figure we'll do that island just south of Index."

Jim unfolded his map from his pocket and stuck a finger on it. "North to south, Paul?"

"That's a for sure."

Jim once again took the time to show me the map, a bay that I would recognize if I came out to it. It was the only place that would look like that.

By the time I was ready, or not, I was out on the fiberglass bow of the Promiscuous Queen. It nudged the shore, and I scuttled over the slick top and a round tube metal rail that wanted to fence me in. Winchester 32 Special in my hand, I did my quickest exit from the boat, trying not to appear too female. In a lot of ways, I had an advantage of not having anything other than my gun. There was no pack to get caught, but the height from the bow of the boat to ground was significant for my short legs. I caught the side of a rock with just my toe and was able to stay upright.

The ground was moist. Moss hung heavily on the rocks and pines nestled in pockets defying gravity. I took surveillance of how to climb the twenty-five-foot incline without disturbing deer or other animals that would give away my presence. Once I reached the top and headed into the bush, I would have to face my fear of getting lost. It had already made its way into the pit of my stomach.

I would do what Jim told me. I would find the tallest tree that set the direction of south and a little west on the pathfinder. I would be constantly looking for that tree to give me direction.

I made my way straight up and sat waiting for the agreed upon twenty minutes, while the others took their positions. It was beautiful up there. Granite rock bulged from the earth, lichen and moss painting the sides of the mosaic. The earthy tones gave me a sense of safety and foundation that can only be felt in the womb. And yet, the bush has always given me significant apprehension. One hundred yards into the forest, I would be immersed in a maze of contours and shapes so vast I could lose sight of where I had been and where I was heading. Whatever intuitive recognition or bearings I might have taken could easily be swallowed in self-doubt and fear. Old fears and old doubts of being surrounded by men that were better than me. Fears and doubts of being alone.

There were days, back when I owned my own construction company, when I felt that fear swell in my belly. Days when I swallowed my fear and kept climbing anyways. Days when I felt lost, but just kept doing.

I remember how the lights on stage shimmered and how terrified I felt. I was attending a Sales and Marketing Award ceremony in Edmonton, Alberta, with a few of my company's submissions in various renovation categories. Sure, I had worked in construction for many years, but I had only been in my own business for a little over a year, and was unrecognizable amidst a host of companies and people that had experience, credibility, and confidence. I was lost in their world; one I hardly knew anything about. I was not only a woman who was not supposed to achieve in this industry, I was among groups of powerful men and their pretty wives that laughed and clinked glasses like they had just finished rounds at the Country Club Golf Course.

I drank to cover up my nervousness. Not enough for me to make a fool of myself, but certainly enough to add a slight numbness to my brain in attempts to bury my fear. The lights and pictures blazed out photographs of contestants of a variety of renovation awards. I was glued to my seat, wearing a multi-colored sequin dress, a blazing smile on my face because this was my moment. The turmoil that lay inside me was hidden from everyone, including the few friends I had asked to join me. Was I good enough?

We won four out of five of the Awards for Best Renovator. When I came off that stage that night, I was high with adrenalin. I was delirious with excitement. My partner, an ex-baseball pitcher from Montana with an Architectural Degree, with his petite sweetheart wife, savored the moment and glory of our young company's achievements. I still felt lost and alone amidst the social network but if my mom could have attended, I knew she would have been proud.

I let that sink in. Regardless of how afraid I was, I just kept doing my best. Here I was in a different world. This time, I was not alone. I had our little Pack. We were back to basics, back to nature, a pure and simple life. After a year of communication and intimacy, I knew deep down that my connection to Jim was strong. The seed had been planted. With nurture, it would survive and grow.

Coming back to earth, the crack of a rifle shot broke the silence. It meant we were to start our "push through the bush." I was central, corralled in the middle so that I would be protected by testosterone. If I veered to one side or the other, I would be herded back into the middle.

I re-checked my compass like we'd practiced. I took a heading on a prominent tree in the distance as reference. The clouds rolled across the sky blocking the sun. I would not be foolishly lost on an island with everyone looking for me. Not this time.

I carefully climbed over fallen spruce trees, big ones, over twelve-inch diameter, being mindful of protruding branches, always looking for that tree that I had put in my compass sight.

I heard shots ring out in succession and they seemed so far ahead of me. I demanded that my legs move faster. I had sunk down to the inside of a ravine, struggling through thickets of underbrush, not able to see much more than ten feet in front of me. A perfect place for any wildlife to hide. I must keep up. There was no point in the chase if I left an open funnel down the middle. I began barking, sounding much like a very scared small dog.

After twenty minutes, the shots had become infrequent. I had moved up on the rise where large pine canopied the earth, eliminating the scrub maple and other underbrush that had impeded my path. I stopped to listen; the sound of my swishing arms and legs abruptly stopped ringing in my ears—like gravel being released from a truck bed. I heard soft rustling followed by the screaming of a territorial squirrel. My compass assured me that I was indeed heading the right direction. In the distance I picked up another movement through the bush, this time larger. I strained to look through gaps of foliage searching for movement that would reveal its presence. There was nothing. I moved on.

After forty-five minutes, I worried that I had once more gotten turned around, perhaps even heading back on my back trail, or perhaps my pace was just too slow. I hoped for the latter. I silently prayed that the clear spaces between the trees was evidence that what lay beyond the tree line was water. A clenching paranoia was only restrained by my mental notes of two men somewhere in the bush with me, sandwiching me in the middle.

I knew I was on the downward slope, which could only mean that the island was coming to an end, levelling off before the shore. I finally broke through the thick underbrush that gnarled its way to the water's edge. Men stood around with solemn, disappointed faces—except for Jim, who was clearly happy at my return. Any deer had safely managed to evade us.

We had not been able to avoid the weather that was now upon us. The wind had been increasing for hours, building five-foot rollers that crested and pounded the Promiscuous Queen as Paul tried to cut through. Even with this sizable craft, Paul was forced to meet the waves head on, and dared not allow the boat to be hit sideward. Its nose rose to meet the swell, sending a spewing geyser over the windshield, soaking us through with frigid lake water. Riding down the other side and crashing into the next. Jim and I were dropped off a couple of miles later. The remaining crew still had over five miles to go before they docked.

Mother Nature provided later that fall. I took down a small buck one early morning as it came for water along a shoreline. Jim was out in a fall blizzard, and a ten pointer came up from behind, planting a front hoof a yard away from his shoulder. Lying on the snow-covered ground, Jim seized the moment when the buck lifted his head to smell the air, just long enough for Jim to make a clean shot and thank the animal for its offering.

We had one more opportunity to see Paul that fall and could not help but ask him why his friend had a name like Wacko. Why would anyone have such a nickname befall them? We had thought it was a rather cruel joke, and inappropriate for a guy that seemed to be pretty normal. Paul explained that he got the name for having clubbed a man to death in a fight. Wacko had just been released from prison for murdering a tourist. It was true. You just never know who you might meet up with in the bush.

CHAPTER 11

SMOKEY

We had first-hand knowledge of why someone was named Wacko, and now we sat across the kitchen table from Smokey. He had done his best with the Servel propane fridge. It was too old for available parts. Maybe it would last, maybe it would not.

With a beer in hand, Paul was content to sit and listen to the story that he had likely heard many times before. Smokey laced his coffee with three heaping teaspoons of sugar and began telling us of his early passage of life on the lake.

"It was probably in about 1930. I'd get out on the lake for two weeks at a time. Three hundred pelts I'd harvest over the winter." He held the cup with both hands, sooty from his work on the fridge.

"My dad did a bit of trapping on our land," I said, "mostly beaver. I think he made a bit of money, but there would be nowhere near that many pelts. What kind of animals did you trap?"

"Oh, there would be beaver alright, but almost everything else as well—otter, fox, mink, muskrat, martin, fisher, raccoon, even skunk and the rare wolf. I didn't like leaving the wife and the kids in winter like that. So much for a woman to have to handle, but it's how it had to be."

He continued, eyes looking at his coffee as though the memories could be found there, eyes that spoke volumes for his 80 years. "She'd fix me up with a pack. All tol' about eight pounds. A tin cup, frying pan, a pot for water and coffee. Lard, a slab of bacon, some pemmican. My woolen blanket. The best of it all was that fruitcake she'd make me. Oh, it was good, filled with walnuts and cherries, and flavored candy. The rest of it was what I needed, a hatchet and knife, some wire for snares. Of course, tobacco and papers."

"My parents both rolled their own," I said. I had memories of watching dad lick the glue on the paper sealing the tobacco into a tightly sealed roll.

Smokey's lips seemed flattened by the constant effort to clench a smoke, like my dad's had been. Smokey had an oversized nose and ears that were out of proportion from the rest of his face. He had probably not been the most handsome of young men. He did have an easy laugh, and his deep brown eyes glimmered with mischief. He had a soft voice like a light breeze on a summer night. I was certain they were traits that kept his family unaware of the hardships that surrounded them.

"Is that how you got your name?" Jim asked.

Smokey chuckled. "Sure is. Don't touch it anymore, but back then I wouldn't be found without one lit up. I could cut down a tree and chop wood and still inhale. I could roll one with one hand. Of course, the tobacco was used for other things. I'd leave at night. Pick a night when the moon was low on the horizon. It would be so cold, it would have a bluish tinge to it, but it was good enough to show me my path. I'd make an offering of tobacco to our grandfathers to help me with my journey."

"So, you are native, Smokey?" I was curious of his background, as my own ancestry was connected to the Swampy Cree in Moose Factory. I was from the John Thomas line from the Hudson's Bay Company. He was the Chief Factor and married a native they simply called Margaret Indian on their marriage certificate.

"I'm Metis."

From there he took us on his journey, and this is how I remember it.

Smokey reached inside a vest pocket for an offering of tobacco. Silently, he asked his grandfathers to guide his journey. It took but moments to secure his pack on his back and his rawhide snowshoes to his moccasin footwear. He set off at a slow shuffling jog, allowing his muscles to stretch. He would need their willingness and stamina in the thirty-mile trek ahead.

They lived on the shores of Lake of the Woods in Northwestern Ontario, in a small native settlement interspersed with Metis. In the summer, steamboats would haul supplies and white visitors, but in the winter the community stood alone in the solitude and cold. Their world was shut off from access for six months or more.

Smokey had been content that he had chosen this night to start his journey. Temperatures had moderated from a deathly cold of -22°F the week previous, to 14°F the last few nights. He didn't know how long it would last, but he only needed eighteen or twenty hours before he would reach his trappers shack in Blueberry Inlet. His shack contained all the necessary traps and dry goods for his stay.

It was a good night for traveling. It was clear, cold, and silent. The silence was a reassurance. It meant no crippling wind or frostbite to his exposed face.

He remembered that the first mile seemed always to be the worst. He merely focused on finding the proper rhythm, lifting his snowshoes that perfect distance that would expend the least effort, leaning his upper body slightly forward to balance the pack weight. Finally, he felt at ease, his body fluid, the *crunch, crunch* of the snow underfoot as rhythmic and precise as a clock ticking. His hot breath left wisps in the night air.

He said he felt he was disappearing into the land and ice, becoming part of its timeless existence. Timeless it was. His forefathers had trapped these waters. They had listened to wendigos and many had been lost in the mists. The great Canadian Shield lay before him in all its magnificence, a wide expanse of flat white, a frozen endless pool abruptly shattered by islands of jagged rock, topped with a forest of giants. He felt moved by the silhouette of spruce and pine against the sky. It reminded him of his daughter's attempts to draw Rusty, their dog, when finally, she would lose patience and try to erase what she had done with a fury of green crayon over the rust brown. How random the lines and curves of nature could be, and yet so perfect.

Smokey had been jogging for four hours when he made his first real stop. Each hour he would slow his pace to a walk for ten or fifteen minutes and then start out again. It would give him a momentary rest, but also allow him to suck back a smoke. He had rolled twenty for the trip, neatly pressed in a candy tin and placed in his breast pocket of his woolen jacket. He had already earned the nickname of Smokey because he was rarely seen without a roll-your-own hanging from the side of his lips.

After four hours, he had chosen to brush away the snow under a stand of young spruce and prepare a temporary resting place. He withdrew the woolen blanket from his pack and wrapped it around himself, covering his head and most of his face. Sitting upright, he dozed off quickly. It was something he had trained himself to do on his trap line. There was never much time to sleep for fear of never waking in the bitter cold. It was best to cat nap every few hours. Stories of men found frozen and half eaten by the wolves and ravens made most young trappers light sleepers.

He awoke a half hour later, feeling the cold gripping him, pain piercing his feet and hands. *Better pain than no feeling*, he thought as he fumbled to get his blanket back into the pack.

He recalled how bitter it was the previous year. It had been one of the coldest winters he could remember. Subsequently, his furs were exceptional. The beaver and otter pelts were thick and shiny like newly polished shoes. There was an extra fifty cents and up to a dollar on every pelt he brought to the fur trader. There was enough extra to purchase the woolen blanket. Hannah, his wife, had insisted after he lost his baby finger to frost bite. The blanket was his most treasured possession and more money than they had ever spent on any one item.

Another four or five hours, and he would eat and rest longer. He sucked on a tiny piece of the fruit cake, letting it thaw and crumble in the well of his cheek, mixing it with his saliva to run freely down his throat like hot syrup. His pace was that of a marathon runner but he had much more at stake. The plaintive howl of a wolf pack reminded him of the many hunters of the night. Occasionally he would see a great grey owl through a window in the trees, or a fox crossing from one island to another. Most animals would do as he did, travel at night when the temperature was the coldest, and rest during the day.

It was nearing daybreak when he built his fire. By now the spot was familiar to him. It was a great massive granite chair that stepped up from the water's edge. Somehow the rock had been sliced in half. It was from the Ice Age he had been told. One half remained as a backdrop, a mystery as to how much of the island it occupied. The other half was the seat of the chair. It had fallen to lie precisely perpendicular.

Each year before he went on, he had taken the time to haul fallen deadfall and starter wood to the base of the rock. It would remain there until the following year. He never knew what he would face in those first ten hours, and it seemed comforting to know what awaited him.

On the rock, Smokey built the biggest, hottest fire that he could. Flames leapt some twenty feet into the sky. With his back to the fire, he made a smaller cook fire, melting snow in his tin pot and a quarter pound of lard in his pan. He threw some coffee grinds in the boiling water and placed the sizzling frying pan off to the side. He cut two thick slices of pemmican and placed them in the hot lard. He then took the bread out in handfuls, cupping as much of the dripping lard as possible and shoveled it into his mouth. The lard tasted salty and rich on the hearty pemmican. He wished he had pepper, but his ravenous appetite was sated. He licked his palm and fingers, his tongue lingering on the stub of the one he had lost. He sat dipping the fruitcake into his black coffee, watching the westerly shore brightening each minute that passed. It was like someone shining a flashlight onto the horizon. To the east, the pink hues of a sunrise had just begun.

With boughs from a red pine, he swept the coals off the base of the rock, carefully inspecting for any live embers that might burn his blanket. The large fire had warmed the rock so that it would hold its heat for three or four hours while he slept. He lay down on the crotch of the rocks, balsam branches for his bed, and hummed a song to the great Mother Earth, content in the knowledge that he had completed half of his journey.

What satisfaction he had felt before he drifted to sleep was lost when he opened his eyes. The sun overhead told him it was early afternoon. He had slept four or five hours and was startled by the changing landscape. The sun was bleached by a winter grey sky. Snow was driven by a fierce wind in sheets of white. The wind gusted and hesitated before exhaling another blast of freezing cold. He was looking through a hazy filter of snow.

It meant only one thing. Whatever the temperature had been, it was now twice or three times colder. Should he sit it out or continue? He could manage to stay where he was for a day or two, living off the rations in his pack. It was unlikely he would snare a rabbit or anything else. In this weather, nothing would move. If it had not been for that missing finger, he would have continued. Smokey, however, could still remember the constant painful reminder of his own flesh freezing, another time when he defied nature's warnings. The rock wall faced south, preventing the northerly winds from reaching him. There was nothing to do but wait.

Smokey kept his fire going, sleeping off and on through the remainder of the day. He would drift in and out of consciousness, hearing the steady roar of the wind through the trees. Finally, around midnight, the wind dropped. As though freed from long-term confinement, he ran as fast as he could for the first mile, then settled back to his rhythmic shuffle.

Smokey was determined to reach his trappers shack by mid-morning. He continued the relentless pace beyond what he himself thought he was capable of, merely slowing to suck back a smoke. By dawn, he had jogged for seven hours with two stops of only twenty minutes apiece. No matter how hard he had tried in those twenty-minute stops, he could do little more than close his eyes. He probably would have noticed the slight discoloration and indentation of the snow had he had those catnaps, but he hit the slush with no notice.

His right snowshoe dropped three inches into slush and he reeled backwards to prevent the other following. He landed on his back, the pack twisting sideways. The wooden frame hit him low on his spine and he felt a stab of pain. He ripped his leather mitts off and tore his moccasin from the iced snowshoe.

Smokey grabbed furiously at the slush and ice that surrounded the webbing on his snowshoe. Within minutes, the slush would be fully frozen. It would slow his progress and possibly even prevent him from reaching the cabin for another night. Another night of exposure to the elements could be life threatening. His hands bled where he had viciously attacked the ice, the crystals sharp as razor edges. He relaxed somewhat as he let the warmth of his hands dissolve the remaining ice on the shoe.

He cursed at himself for being so careless. He knew there was very little room for mistakes in the northern climate. The slush covered an area as far as he could see, no mistaking its greyish tinge below the surface of snow. When it stuck to the snowshoe it became a leaden weight. He withdrew a smoke, dragging long and hard on it, pondering his next move. The slush appeared as a vast obstacle in his path. No guarantees, but usually the cracks that allowed the water to settle on the ice in the first place started from some shore. For this reason, he started off towards the largest part of the bay, even though the nearby islands offered him shelter.

Smokey concentrated on remaining calm and alert. His anxiousness to reach his destination could have cost him a limb or even his life. His wife and children depended on him, and he must return in one piece. He settled back into his methodical pace, forgetting the cold and his weariness. A mile or so out, he saw three deer picking their way across the bay, heading towards a large island. They were on the move now that the weather had cleared, but more importantly they too would not choose passing through slush. They were no more than a half a mile away.

The slush ended some two hundred yards off where the deer had traveled. Smokey turned and headed south again. The detour cost him a few hours, but he still could make his camp by dusk.

The last leg of his journey he spent in reflection. This vast land he lived in provided everything he needed. Its harsh winters gave him a good livelihood. It was bountiful, with fresh water, clean air, and an abundance of food. The great spirit of his ancestors unveiled their wisdom to him through nature. Every living thing, plant and animal contained all of life's secrets. It was necessary only to listen. It was as simple as the birch tree that provided medicine and forewarned of storms. The bark was gentle enough to be brewed for old age pains, yet strong enough to carry hunters in canoes and wise enough to turn its leaves upwards to meet the rains. Smokey knew that all of life's lessons could be learned from nature.

In the distance, Smokey could make out the snowy outline of his trapper's shack. The last rays of sunlight painted the sky with hues of soft pinks and purples. He thought about his children. He would show them this place some day. He hoped he could also pass on some of the lessons this land of lakes had taught him.

Aside from refreshing his coffee cup, we let Smokey tell his tale uninterrupted. We were captivated, not only by the incredible history of the area, but the brutal forces that he and others endured in the far north. It made our experience trivial in comparison. Smokey left that night, wrinkled and weathered with a twinkle in his eye. We watched him go, engulfed by the faint shadows of nightfall, a rhythmic dance in his walk, with no more weight to carry.

CHAPTER 12

THE PURPLE TOBOGGAN

Sekima had grown. In his first year he had reached eighty-five pounds. Jim had worked him with some basic commands to haul dead wood from the center of our island on our plastic purple toboggan. Sekima learned to be patient while Jim loaded, and then on command he would follow Jim, who ran in front.

Life on the island was evolving at a very slow pace, but with enormous change and many lessons. Our happiness with the simple life was because of a natural kindred spirit with nature and also because of our strong desire to make it work. We were determined and trusted our instincts. We had willingness to heed lessons. Ultimately, we would need all of those to survive. But when it came to Sekima, our third family member, we could only trust him to a point.

Finally, there was freeze-up over the big waters of Whitefish Bay in late December. There was sufficient ice, at least three inches to be able to walk the four miles to town. There had been no contact with anyone since late November when the bays froze and boats were removed from the waters. Our little red boat had been placed in storage with the marina, and Joe had returned us to our island with a final wave. We were alone on the island, and there was no more contact with the outside world.

So it was that we were excited for this last-minute trip over the ice to mainland before Christmas. It would mean that we would have fresh vegetables, so long as they did not freeze on our return. A small cooler would hopefully insulate tender leaves and Christmas traditions. We had missed salads for over a month. But this trip meant lettuce, peppers, and mushrooms. It meant cabbage, carrots, onions, yams, and squash. It meant on Christmas Day we could prepare traditional coleslaw, mashed potatoes with yams. And of course, turkey that could stay frozen in our natural freezer of the outdoors. We no longer needed an indoor freezer compartment. The outdoor insulated, abandoned refrigerator that had never been removed from the island was perfect storage for our meat and fish. The temperatures were well below what a freezer compartment needed.

The trip to town would also mean we would be able to receive Christmas cards and presents that I knew would have arrived from family and friends. It was my understanding that most of the time there was no ice until after Christmas across the big waters of Whitefish Bay, or the ice was likely not safe for walking before Christmas. A solid three inches was a blessing for our first winter.

The purple plastic toboggan had cost five dollars. For me, the happy feature of the toboggan was its color. Purple was my favorite. We had drilled two holes on its front lip and attached two fine ropes that extended to the traces of Sekima's harness. We would cross-country ski the four miles to town and let Sekima pull the toboggan. The desolate expanse of lake would keep him in check. A white expanse flattened to the horizon in all directions. As we got close to mainland, we would tie a rope around his thick linked chain collar to ensure that he was not tempted by people or places.

Things went pretty well as planned, without incident, until we started our journey home.

"We're going to have to put some things in our packs." I anxiously watched as Sekima struggled under the weight of the toboggan, which was now loaded with Christmas presents and groceries, stacked high and tied down with binder twine.

"It's not too much for him," Jim said.

"But the snow keeps bunching in front of the toboggan. It's too much weight for him and the toboggan." I felt so bad for him. He was young, and trying so hard. The toboggan, weighted down with goods, burrowed rather than slid.

"I'm telling you. He's fine. He's pulled much heavier loads of wood on the island." Jim wasn't ready to give in to my motherly instincts. Sekima had been pulling an easy two to three hundred pounds of stacked wood for Jim as they pulled deadfall on the island to add to our existing wood for winter.

Sekima pulled a few more yards and sat down on his huge haunches. The dog's excessive exertion to pull the toboggan was largely due to the number of times he was stopping and starting. In order to start from a standstill, he had to jump numerous times against the traces, front chest straining in mid-air before the toboggan would slide above the fluffy deep snow. He was early in his training. He did not understand life's teachings. It is easier to keep things going once the momentum is there. I lingered back with Sekima, coaxing him, while Jim skied ahead of us.

"Come on, good boy. You can do it. Let's go, let's go." All the familiar words that he knew to no avail. He was quitting, little by little.

Our path across the barren ice was calculated as the shortest distance to our island. Once we were away from mainland, we made our way due west past several islands over a mile away from our direct course. At this slow pace we would make it home at dusk. It was already after three p.m. The sun was hanging low and heavy in the western sky, bruised reddish hues already coating the tree line with heavy sleepy eyes. Silence enveloped us. It is a silent time of the year, stillness in a quiet bubble with dramatic, fluid colors. When animals lie dormant, skies empty of birds and trembling leaves are long encased in snow. On the horizon, the hues of magenta turn to Payne's grey awaiting a shower of Northern lights. Broken silence during the wintery night when Mother Nature encapsulates you with whispers in your ears.

Two whitetail deer vaulted off one of the islands, white tail flags bouncing with every jump. Whether chased by wolves or some other disturbance, they were heading to another island, and they were within Sekima's peripheral vision. I saw them at approximately the same time. They were cutting a path perpendicular to ours and behind islands we had already passed. Without hesitation or warning, Sekima broke out in full pursuit, toboggan and all. I screamed for him to stop. He kept running flat out. The deer had a tremendous lead on Sekima, but Sekima was on a quest. Having heard the commotion behind him, Jim was quick to add his loud command for Sekima to stop. Our voices echoed off the rocks and had no effect.

By now we had skied to each other and stood in dismay as our suddenly energetic dog bounded across the windblown, drifting snow.

"Tired dog, alright," Jim said, disgusted.

"A bit of a surprise," I meekly responded.

"If he gets that harness or toboggan stuck on that island, he can stay there until he figures it out."

"Oh no." I saw how far he had run. The distance was beyond my energy. I was reminded of how physically weak I'd felt when I'd gotten lost.

We watched as the deer bounded up the side of the island and out of sight. Sekima made it to the base of the island moments later. The deer were already long gone. They not only had a lead of about a half mile, but they were much faster than any dog—save for perhaps a greyhound without a purple toboggan. There was no lone predator that would take a deer easily. Even wolves hunting in packs developed a deliberate plan of attack, approaching only the weak, old, or young deer.

Sekima was clearly visible, struggling to climb the side of the island. His efforts were futile. Most islands rose steeply, thirty to forty degrees. He made it about twenty feet up the slope.

"Jim, he's stuck. We have to go get him."

"He's over a mile away, in the wrong direction from home. We can't do that," he said flatly, knowingly.

"Sekima! Sekima! Sekima!" I followed my yells with a piercing whistle.

Jim took up the chant as we watched helplessly from a distance. Sekima appeared to have the purple toboggan twisted sideways on the slope. He had not been able to move further up the slope, so it was likely he had gotten hung up on a piece of deadfall with his loaded toboggan. It was just too much for the young malamute.

Finally losing interest in the deer, Sekima heard our urgent calls. We watched his final attempt to change directions to retreat down the slope, fighting the lodged purple toboggan.

"Sekima come! Let's go! Let's go! Sekima!" Jim's deep voice echoed off the islands.

Suddenly the toboggan broke loose, sliding sideways off the incline. With one big leap, Sekima was on the snow-covered ice again. At barely a trot, he veered towards us, a small dog form pulling a bright purple toboggan. From this distance, it appeared there were still some packages attached.

"Oh, what a relief," I sighed.

"Maybe for him. He could have stayed there for all I care. He doesn't listen when he's called."

I was pretty sure that Jim would not have left him. Even so, retrieving him would have added time that we did not have. Darkness would set in, and temperatures would plunge the predicted -13°F. Jim had already started to ski away, not willing to waste any more time and confident that Sekima was well-equipped to make the return. Although still anxious about the condition of my Christmas presents, I realized Sekima would catch up. We made our way across the sprawling landscape of shadows. A man leading, a woman some distance behind, and, bringing up the rear, a dog with a purple toboggan.

CHAPTER 13

WINTER NIGHTS

Neither of us had ever spent a Christmas quite like this. When I was growing up, spruce tree fragrance floated through the air. Sparse in ornaments, the Christmas tree was coated with shiny tinsel. Christmas Eve would be freezing cold but the tiny church adorned with nativity scenes and song brought joy to my heart, as well as my family. There were not many gifts on Christmas morning, but the food was plenty. Into adulthood Christmas became less tradition, more parties, and more presents.

For both Jim and I, it was a wondrous Christmas on the island. We had made decorations for a limp—but not lifeless—Charlie Brown balsam tree, by painting foam remnants from the aerosol cans Jim used to seal air leaks. The decorations were a variety of shapes and forms of painted foam. The aerosol cans with straw spouts were great for small spaces, but the foam tended to expand and bubble once it had filled a crack. It was from these overflows that we cut and created our Christmas figurines. Our creativity was endless—from tiny Santas and reindeer to delicate songbirds on branches laden with snow. Jim had volumes of acrylic paint and the abstract forms of the foam let us explore a variety of creations. To add texture, we picked large, open, white pinecones from the forest floor and painted the tips of the individual pedals. Having a fondness for the tiny shrews that initially occupied the cabin, we recreated their little bodies, with pointy noses and long tails of grey yarn, using the smaller jack pine cones that had already lost their seeds. The seedless cones took on a fluffy quality that resembled our grey, furry visitors.

Our winter evenings had become rituals. With dusk fast approaching by four p.m., I would start dinner preparation under natural light much earlier. Coal oil lanterns provided meagre illumination for food preparation and cooking, and even the old Servel propane refrigerator had no interior lights. It was always best to use the wood heater for cooking to conserve our propane. For that reason, most meals consisted of slow-cooker type recipes, stews and roasts, baked navy beans, fish casseroles and chili. We relied heavily on venison, ruffed grouse, fish, dried legumes, rice and pasta as our staples. Vegetables were canned.

The cherry-stained lacquered plank table had bark edging and was barely big enough for a setting of four. There was only two. Our conversations over dinner centered around weather, chores, and more weather based on what we had to do.

At the end of the day, we sat in the soft light of the lanterns, the clear doors of the heater allowing the dancing flames to warm our minds. We would sit reading and writing for several hours in sagging armless chairs with animal print covers left behind by the former owners. Jim kept an ongoing diary of the weather and work to be done, while I wrote of sights and sounds of nature that held me spellbound. Grizzly, alternative medicine author Deepak Chopra, Trail of the Wolf, a full Zane Grey Collection were all at our disposal for reading.

CHAPTER 14

THE TOTEM

I looked up from my book to watch the spiral coil of flames through the glass door of the heater. I cocked my head from side to side. The beautiful majestic head of a wolf, ears erect, was etched in the granite wall of the fireplace. Its piercing eyes stared at me. I rolled my head again, from side to side, and the imagine remained and became even clearer. "Look, Jim," I whispered, for fear it would hear me and disappear.

"Hmmm," he mumbled, undisturbed.

"Look at the fireplace granite, Jim. What do you see?" I urgently engaged him, hoping the symbol would not disappear. The wolf spirit was a bond we shared. The first gift I had ever given Jim was that of a beautiful figurine of the alpha male and female together standing tall on a slab of granite. Their muzzles lightly touched, and it was called "The Wolf Kiss." The wolf spirit represented both strength of individuality and commitment of the most serious and unshakable kind. It was the reason that we had chosen to name our island in an aboriginal word that meant "daughter of the wolf."

"What?" He looked up from his book.

"Look. Do you see anything on the face of the granite?"

"Not particularly."

I feared that if I got up to point it out, the wolf image would disappear. But I also had to prove it to myself. That it was not just the flickering light of the kerosene lamp playing tricks on me. I rose, slowly moving towards the shadow that seemed to be watching me. I could feel myself trembling as I drew the outline of the wolf's head with my index finger.

"Here. Can you see it now? It's a wolf head. The elongated nose, the ears."

"Sort of, I guess."

I knew by his lack of enthusiasm, that he was not seeing the image that was still so vividly clear. Regardless, I could not help but share my excitement. "I thought it was just a reflection from the coal oil lanterns at first. But it hasn't gone away. It's right here." I held the palm of my hand directly over the wolf face, feeling the warmth radiating from the granite. "It's such a good omen."

"It sure is." He smiled up at me.

I was overwhelmed with gratitude and love. It was so wonderful to be with a man who wanted me to be happy and did not judge or doubt me. Shortly after that the image faded, but its symbol from my life never did.

Jim, too, had had experiences with wolves that were symbolic of his kindred spirit with them. He had told me of one encounter in particular. He had been hunting elk in the mountains outside of Canmore, Alberta. The snow was heavy beyond the tree line, and considerably colder. He retreated to his spike camp early afternoon, over the ridge of the west face valley just below the snow line. He gathered wood and set up his sleep tent in front of a large rock that would have absorbed heat during the day.

He had seen no animals, only tracks, and had heard a pack of wolves during the day. It was a full moon. The night promised to be clear, cold, and dead calm. By four o'clock, dusk was upon him, so he built his fire and made a supper, heating a can of stew on a small propane burner. He would keep the fire going as long as possible to stay warm. After eating, he sat, going over his strategy for traversing the mountain and finding the herd the following day. Between eight and nine p.m., he suddenly saw animal eyes beyond the fire. His initial thought was that they were deer, but the eyes were too low to the ground. At the edge of the clearing, about a hundred yards away, he thought he saw a wolf, but then it disappeared. Another hour or so, and he saw multiple eyes. It was the Pack. One of the wolves came within fifty yards and then the others followed. They came closer, within twenty-five yards, and lay down. Once in a while, one would get up and lie down again. Perhaps they were interested in the warmth of the fire, perhaps they were curious, or liked the lingering smell of stew. He felt no threat but a comfort in their presence, as though for some short time, he had been included in their community. At about eleven, he got into his tent and lay on his stomach, looking out. They were still there. He awoke at three or four in the morning. The fire was out. His breath was illuminated by the moon and stars. They were gone.

Although we had different stories, we had similar connections and beliefs about wolves. We both believed that the wolf was intelligent, that wolves formed a faithful community for their young and elderly, that they hunted and killed for survival and not sport. Theirs is a noble sacrifice to the family unit. Depicted as loners, they are highly family orientated, teaching their young not to overkill, taking the lowest grade or weakest of animals as their prey. Photos have displayed the most elderly setting the pace at the front of a long line of wolves as they travel, so as not to put them at risk of falling behind. To understand their community is to have experienced the faithfulness and devotion and unconditional trust of a dog. Wolves have been vastly misunderstood by the general public. Their faithfulness and devotion are to their own families. The alpha male and female remain together, for better or for worse, for their lifetime. The Pack remains strong.

It seems sad in so many ways that some humans do not show

the same intelligence, nor demonstrate the same commitment to children or elderly. Working parents with less motivation and energy to teach their children basic life skills, adopting an attitude that the responsibility lies with educators or technology. Children growing up to be disconnected from parents, with no desire or compelling reason to care for the aging, the parent who is now the elder. Of course, this is a greatly simplified version of a complex set of problems, however, with the same result. That Pack is fragmented and weak.

CHAPTER 15

SHORT DAYS, LONG NIGHTS

Winter was fully upon us—shorter days and longer periods of intense cold. Cutting the birch logs in pieces to be split was a formidable chore. Coated in clay and sand, every cut dulled Jim's chainsaw blade so that he had to stop and sharpen frequently. The task itself was not only immense in frigid temperatures, but painfully slow and arduous. This was survival—he had to continue.

Days of cold and frustration seeped into our lives as Jim fought to find a way to channel his aggravation. I found him outside one day, sawing through coated birch logs, cursing lawyers that had sat on his Board of Directors with his public company. He blamed them for constantly wanting him to minimize their risk and exposure, shackling him with opinions without guidance. I worried about him. *What was he doing living in the past? Why was he thinking about this now in this brutal cold?*

I knew each cut was a painful reminder of how difficult life can be when thrown with a coating of dirt. It suddenly came to me. Whether conscious or not, Jim was fueling himself to continue by using his anger. There was no other solution to the stack of logs that lay before him. There was only one way to do this— it was to cut away that tough layer.

Icicles dripped off the roof edge, some of them so long that they melded with the mountain of snow around us. We shoveled narrow paths to the log pile, the outhouse, and the boathouse. Our weekly ritual of showers, a VCR movie, popcorn, and Pepsi was always viewed as a luxury. So far, our system was working. The line with the internal bladder was functioning the way it was designed. The ice thickness in the boathouse was growing considerably, but foam placed in the opening that covered the water prevented serious ice from forming.

Daytime temperatures hovered at -6°F and dipped to -31°F at night. We were quickly running out of propane, as the Servel was very inefficient. We anticipated that we would need to ski to mainland with an empty sixty-pound propane bottle and refill, however, the snow was deep and it would be difficult traversing. We waited. The buzz of ice augers the first week of January was both a surprise and a relief. We were no longer alone on the lake, and we could start moving from the island again. We had taken short excursions from the island, but there was no urgency to go anywhere.

Our location on Whitefish Bay, with waters from sixty to 250 feet deep, were ideal for sports fisherman from the US border states. So, when the group arrived, I quickly skied out with Sekima to their location, a group of five men, snow machines and all the toys that go with a winter vacation in Canada—ice augers, GPS, depth finders, and sleds. The one thing they did not have was hot blueberry pie made that morning. I made my invitation to the friendliest of the men, to visit for hot coffee and blueberry pie. They came, two brothers from Brainard, MN. They came because they were cold, shivering inside their full snow machine suits, full head gear, and elbow length gloves. Their enthusiasm had waned with winds from the northwest blowing snow in their faces and freezing ice to fishing lines. It was so cold. With wind chill it felt like -50°F on the skin. Fish were not biting, but the frost was.

The men were curious and amazed at our lifestyle, envious of our pristine location, a fishing location they considered a paradise. They were in no hurry to join their group that they could see now from our front room. By the time they left, they had insisted that they would take our propane tank in on their sled and return it first thing in the morning. It was a blessing, and Sekima was relieved of a heavy purple toboggan adventure.

Shortly after their delivery, we returned to town for mail and fresh items, skiing on freshly made snowmobile trails. Sekima could fly along the trails with the purple toboggan behind him. We no longer allowed his earlier freedom. I used my cross-country skis and held two long nylon ropes. My main lead was attached to his harness that V-shaped over his back. The other was attached to his chain collar. I was much smaller than Jim, closer to the ground, and had better agility to recover my balance. Not only could Sekima pull me quickly, but the uneven snow machine tracks that often zig zagged across each other were brutally difficult to maneuver. My skis would cross, or be thrown sideways over the uneven surface. The upside was the effortlessness of being pulled. I was along for the ride. Sekima was now more familiar with basic commands, but the lead on his chain collar was our reassurance that he would not bolt after a deer or snow machine.

That first year, the buzz of a snow machine was both an irritant and exercise for Sekima. He became a bit of a folkloric character as fisherman, typically from the south side of the border, took sightings of a lone wolf chasing their snow machines. He would come charging down from the top of an island. Lucky for them their machines were faster than he.

Sekima had become accustomed to pulling, and he had gained incredible muscle and weight. It was easier for me to handle him behind the sled than walking beside him. He regularly took me for a playmate, someone that he could ambush, throw his full broad chest straight at me, hit me hard, knock me down, and run around me in circles, totally out of reach, and totally out of control. He was indeed an alpha male.

We learned very early of his dominance. Jim frequently had to grab him by the scruff of the neck and hold him to the ground to demonstrate who was the Pack leader. Jim finally caught him in the act of knocking me down one day. He grabbed him with two large hands around his neck and forced him to the ground. He was never hurt, never whined or whimpered, but grew to learn that he was not the alpha of this Pack.

When we used the purple toboggan, he was attentive to command. I would frequently have to call on him to stop, a "whoa Sekima," and, if necessary, pull on the harness with a tug. I did not use the chain link collar but I knew if the alpha male malamute decided to run for it, I did not want to be along for the ride. We needed to stop frequently because our pace was so much faster than Jim's. No one could physically keep up cross-country skiing behind Sekima and our purple toboggan.

There were endless days of bitter cold. Frost etched on window panes like spider webs and dreamcatchers. Merciless northwest-erlies blew for days at a time, making outdoor activities largely impossible. We huddled inside, the big fireplace and the cookstove, the PIG, running constantly. We had moved our bed from the open loft next to the fireplace. It was not only appreciably warmer but easier for Jim to add wood in the middle of the night.

It was a period of hibernation, of meditation, complete darkness by four p.m., with just a hint of sunrise by eight. Our exterior insulation on the walls and roof was superior to the average home, but our floor remained uninsulated, and our cabin windows were single pane. We had closed off a rear bedroom and used it for cold storage. We had plastic film on the smaller windows. The front windows, where we sat for most of the day, gave us a full view of the west. We had cut three-inch polystyrene panels to fit snugly inside the window trim at dark. The days were short. The evenings long as we waited.

CHAPTER 16

ICE ROAD

Paul was one of those people that thrived on helping people who he considered as eccentric as he, or in desperate need, but that was not all of him. He would also respond to high-risk situations, akin to a firefighter that feels the excitement to fight the extreme blaze, or a storm chaser after the big tornado. There was no doubt that if you were in trouble on the lake, you would want Paul looking for you. He would be out there first and take serious risks on the lake. He would take bigger risks than local rescue. And so, we had Paul looking out for us, as he considered us in trouble, in his mind. There was good reason for that. Islands were seasonal respites. There were no permanent residents that would consider island dwelling. There were no local residents that considered it sensible. There were too many downsides. Too many unfavorable aspects— like no people, no phone, no road, no television, no flush, nowhere.

Paul ran a very successful barge business that included construction, and part of his job was being charming, being a good storyteller, and billing island customers for what he considered a fair but profitable margin. There was a distinct difference in his relationships, and we came to learn the difference.

He arrived shortly after the snowmobilers, shortly after we made our first trip to town. It was a Suburban—orange, with a seven-foot-wide plow. It was midday and it made a wide sweep in front of our boathouse and stopped short. An exuberant Sekima recognized Paul with happy bounds. I cannot say that I was not exuberant, but I had mixed feelings as well. A road to town. A means of driving whenever we wanted to would mean other people in our lives.

But where and why are we going anywhere? We wanted to be nowhere with no one but ourselves. We had been extensively outgoing; both of us had sales and marketing backgrounds, and our businesses required it. Both of us rose to the occasion to become leaders in more than one capacity. We had always been on the stage for this or that.

A stage can be an uncomfortable, draining place to be. There is a high fostered by the adrenalin that pumps through your veins as you motivate and stimulate others. There is a depletion of energy afterwards, a need to regroup and regain, like after a party that you have thrown, or an extended family meal. A lawyer that pours energy into their final statements. A talking head that has to convince you nightly. A stand-up comedian who requires you to laugh. A mother or father constantly trying to prove their parenting skills. When it is time to feed the soul, it is time to reorganize life. And that is what this was all about. We were protective of that very thing—our isolation.

It was a relief for that first year not to have the constant pressure of business. A big relief. But we needed a way of making a living off the island all year round. We needed to work or our small reserves would be eaten up. We paid nothing for this diversion of the ice road for Paul. He was practically passing by us anyways, as he had told us earlier. Paul was having fun on the lake. Paul was looking out for us. How could we resist? Paul was establishing our dependency on him.

"Yoah. How you been?" He swatted at Sekima as the malamute ran in giant circles around him.

We had made our way down to where he had parked the Suburban. It was a bit astonishing for both us. We had not anticipated being off the island until the ice broke up in spring. And here we were with a road!

"I've only made a single pass, so I'll be at this a few days yet."

"But that's it. We are connected to mainland!" I said excitedly.

"You are at that. Thought you might want to get to town, but the ice has been slow to form up."

We told him that we had made it into town once to pick up some mail and fresh items, and that we'd had snowmobilers get us a refill on one of our propane tanks

"Well, now you can just do it with your truck, right to the island." His lips curled into a smile, but he rarely showed his teeth. "Wouldn't happen to have a beer, would you?"

We had the same amount of beer since the fall. Neither one of us were beer drinkers in the winter.

"I'm pretty sure, and they're on the cabin floor so they should be pretty cool."

"Just one for the road would be good."

It seemed a small price to have road delivery. As Jim and Paul continued to exchange thoughts, I hurried up the steps and found a beer. Beer in hand, already opened, he was gone, his plow kicking up another swath of snow.

Several days later, there was a ribbon the width of a private runway, a one-hundred-foot-wide ice road that connected us to mainland. Paul had explained the reasons for its span. There was less than six inches of snow in some places, as it had been wind swept towards shorelines. That was nowhere near what would accumulate over the winter. Eventually those banks would get deeper and thicker and unmovable for the plow, making the road less wide. The more critical issue was the wind. Strong, vicious northwesterly winds would be ongoing, sweeping the snow like tumbleweed across the plains, dropping on the inner banks of the road reducing its width to a wagon trail by the spring. The one hundred feet in width was a good start.

The ice road brought good and bad. It was good that we could drive back and forth, no differently than someone would on a regular road, except for storms that stopped driving for a few days. We did not care. We rarely went out more than once every two weeks, but at least we could. The bad part was that people were curious about ice roads. They were not local people. They were visitors. They thought the road was provided by a public service. When it ended at our island, they did not know what to do. They parked. Likely admiring the landscape. It wreaked havoc on our quiet peace. It wreaked havoc for Sekima.

CHAPTER 17

KIDNAPPED

I still had some business dealings in Edmonton, and the ice road gave me good reason not to put them off any longer. Jim would stay on the island with Sekima and tend to the fires. I drove to Winnipeg and took the short flight to Edmonton. I would be back in a few days.

Sekima was kept inside during my departure, and Jim kept an eye on him all morning as he worked outside. Sometime between three and four p.m., Sekima disappeared, likely trying to follow me, or just on a trip of his own. By the time Jim noticed him missing, it was dark. He called, whistled, and no Sekima. He had no vehicle, and no way of knowing where he would have gone. He would have to wait.

He was relieved by mid-morning the next day. A local drove out on the ice road, asking if our dog was missing. There was a dog in town that had come home with his kids, who had been at a bonfire where they were cooking hot dogs. Apparently, the dog had eaten a few and followed them home. They did not know what to do, so they put him in the garage. They were looking for his owner. A few inquiries in town led them to believe he might be our malamute.

Sekima had no boundaries and had already become a bit of an icon. He had spiraled a panic for some locals that first saw him. They had used our ice road to bring them closer to a trout hole.

They saw him coming. The snow had become hardened, it crusted on top and could carry his weight. He came across the barren field of snow at full speed, great strides, a wolf-grey, with incredible speed and fluency. They ran to their truck and rolled up their windows. He stopped at their truck, looking up, curled malamute tail wagging his happiness. And then they realized, saw his dog collar and his friendly disposition.

Black Jack was one of those that came out regularly, choosing his favorite trout hole, happy that we had an ice road. It was usually only in spring or with a snow machine that you could venture out onto Whitefish Bay. The ice road gave Black Jack freedom. Black Jack was a local. A Metis, born and raised, who lived off the lake as much as he could. He was the one that told us that someone would shoot Sekima because he looked like a wolf.

He brought his little black fish shack and plunked it off our ice road within a half mile from our island. Sekima visited routinely. There were cheezies and cheese sandwiches. There were likely strokes and scratches and long discussions and stories of the Windigos that Sekima should be careful of as Black Jack drank his Crown Royal and deliberated about the state of affairs throughout the north. And then Sekima would come home, never letting on of his interaction.

But then one day he did not come home. It was a sunny day, and he was never gone long. He had a job to do, and that was largely protection of the island and our Pack. He could not be gone long. The alpha male instinct would compel him to return. We both questioned his length of time away at the same time. Where is he? What happened? We had not seen him for several hours. Initially, we used the piercing referee whistle that he would hear from a far distance. We stood down by the deck waiting to see him against the stark white of the landscape. It was cold and still, an empty unmoving background.

Dusk was just around the corner. It was already three. We drove out to Black Jack's fish hut. He was still there. He said he had seen him much earlier in the day. He and his boy Sekima had their traditional lunch, and the dog left as usual. He had not seen which way he'd gone. He was about ready to leave himself.

We had brought our binoculars and had been careful to watch for tracks in softer drifts that might provide us with a direction. We had little to go on. We kept going, knowing, however unlikely, he may have decided to follow the ice road towards mainland. Perhaps a deer, or a dog. Perhaps a wolf pack. Perhaps we had once again trusted him too far. We knew it was our fault. We had no way of fencing the island, and had chosen to monitor his comings and goings as best we could.

I had my window open, intensely studying the white expanse and checking shadowed shorelines of islands while Jim drove and took sight in the distance. I saw a group of fishermen off to the south who had set up fish shacks off an ice road that intersected with ours. It was a small group, perhaps four or five, and then suddenly from behind one of the trucks, I was alerted to what appeared to be a dog.

"Wait. I think I see something."

"Where?"

"Where those guys are fishing. Stop so I can get a better look." I strained to get a better look at the dog that was meandering around the trucks and men.

"It's him." I passed the binoculars to Jim. He agreed. It was a big dog. Curly tail.

We were there within minutes. Jim got out of the truck. I could hear them. Sekima joyfully greeting him.

"Hi. Where did he come from?" Jim asked.

"Saw him running across from that direction." One of the fishermen pointed west. Not towards the ice road, but directly west towards our island. They were all dressed in full dark snow suits, winter beanies or toques. Aside from various heights, they were almost indistinguishable, with sun glasses to cut the glare from the snow reflection, and a few days of beard growth.

"Good looking dog. He's been hanging around. Friendly," another offered.

"He's my dog," Jim stated flatly. Sekima was already racing around Jim affectionately greeting him.

"Oh, we didn't know where he came from. Didn't know, maybe abandoned."

"Let's go, Sekima."

Without hesitation, Sekima trotted to our truck, ready for his ride home.

"Not a good idea to befriend a dog in this community. Not good to encourage him with food to stick around. You never know what sadness it might bring to a family's children when their dog doesn't come home. Worse yet, it might agitate some parent. There's no reason to think that's it's not somebody's pet."

"He just showed up. No offense man." The shortest gestured with open hands.

"No offense taken. Just giving you some good advice." Jim was done with them. He wanted them to understand that there would have been consequences if they had decided to take him.

Sekima was ready to come home. Jubilant and no doubt finished with his excursion, he jumped quickly into the truck. We suspected that they had been fishing on our ice road, and had taken Sekima with them. It made more sense than Sekima traveling over three miles across open windswept snow. They would not have anticipated someone living out on the lake. Sekima was a beautiful grey-brown malamute with that distinctive mask, in his full coat of winter colors, like a fall arrangement, healthy and hefty. There would be every reason that someone would want to rescue him.

And no doubt when Jim arrived, they realized he had a family. We would never know for sure how Sekima got there. He had a mind of his own. But he was found.

He wore a harness from then on, with an orange flag, our names and where we lived taped to it. We had thought about it before, when Black Jack said he might get mistaken for a wolf and shot. At that time, we had decided not to, weighing the risk of him getting shot versus getting the harness entangled in brush and stuck. We had determined the latter was too much of a risk. We had waited, but now the time had arrived.

CHAPTER 18

BREAK UP

Paul visited many times over the winter. We were always on his way. We welcomed his visits, and he welcomed that we had some beer.

Spring was near. It had been an uneventful winter for us. The ice road had been wiped out at times by drifting snow and slush. When there is no one and nothing, there is no anxiety, no urgency, and life takes on a beat with nature. Days blend into months, following the light and the dark, following the rhythm and cycle of the seasons.

The ice remained the thickest on the ice road, driven like frost into the ground. It also remained solid around our island with our north and westerly exposure. But the bay and landing that connected us to mainland was deteriorating with its southern exposure. It also had more traffic from snow machines, ATVs, and 4-wheel drive trucks that took advantage of a short period of time in the spring they could go free-wheeling. There was no snow, and for those who were familiar with the lake, they could go many places, largely for fishing, or to do spring work on island properties, building docks, burning deadfall, or simple maintenance.

Gradually, the ice closest to the shoreline broke away, and it was not long before we once again were alone on the lake. We were locked onto our island by a rim of open water. Our truck was on mainland. Our boat would be our next mode of transportation.

We watched as the sun rose higher in the sky on a daily basis. Watched as the sunsets extended and deepened their orange hues. Watched as the ice went dark, then the chalky white of rotting crystal, and finally returned to a black mat that signaled the ending of its existence. Rivulets of water like stream currents sprung up during the heat of the day, slicing the expanse into large chunks that floated together and then apart with shifting winds. And then the rain came, flushing frost from the earth and spreading a blanket of dense fog where it met the frigid ice and water. It came quietly at first, and then finally in torrents with wind that swept the fog away. It came from the west, driving huge chunks of ice down the channel called Barney's Narrows. The open water in front of the boathouse and part of our bay was filled with drifting chunks. We watched with alarm as the steady flow of ice pushed and churned together, toppling together, the weaker ones crushed, compacting and solidifying into a solid mass. The void was being filled, nowhere else to go. The boathouse trembled in its midst; the bottom foot of plywood was sliced away from the frame with perfect diamond cutter precision.

When it was finally over, we sighed with relief. The next day we could see the damage, but we had survived the worst. The rain had pulverized weaker sections of ice, and others drifted like molten lava, plenty of room to weave around the islands. Sekima took to jumping from ice flow to ice flow near the shore, shaking his head with pleasure and delight.

Just when we thought it was over, the ice reconnected, like old friends rekindling relationships. We awoke to our northerly shore melded, a puzzle of ice flows pushed solidly together, allowing Sekima one more to rendezvous to the neighboring island, towards tantalizing smells of things dead and decaying.

We watched him from the dock. As he neared the island's shoreline, he crashed through the ice. He started paddling. As he did, the gap widened. The ice was spoiled by the spring, crumbling beneath him. He was too far from shore. His attempts to get footing were failing.

I felt helpless and frantic. "Jim he can't get up onto the ice!"

"It's been only a minute or two. He'll be fine, he just has to get some solid ice."

I waited what seemed an eternity, fear rising in my voice. "We can't wait any longer. How can we help him?"

"Damn. Go get my life jacket, a rope, and the needle bar. I can try to take the canoe across to get him."

I returned, and Jim had already placed the aluminum canoe on the shore. He would walk as far as he risked and then try to break the ice with the needle bar to get to Sekima. It was a heavy metal bar, pointed at the end. Again, that nauseating pit in my stomach of things out of control in an instant. Crying inside and pleading with God to help us.

Jim was putting himself at risk. If he fell through himself, he likely had thirty to sixty minutes himself before hypothermia set in. I would be helpless to do anything but watch. I glanced again at Sekima, swimming wider sweeps now in the hole he had made.

The rope and needle bar were in the canoe. Jim handed me his coat and put the life jacket on. He gently pushed the aluminum canoe in front of him and took a few hesitant steps on the ice.

"He's up! He's on the ice!" I cried. Sekima had found a stronghold on solid ice and had pulled himself out. We watched as he took a few steps, shook his himself from head to tail, water spiraling around him. He bounded towards us as though it was an everyday occurrence. We both knelt and brought him into our arms, wet fur and water droplets hiding our tears.

He had amazing strength and endurance. A dog is a dog, right? No, not this dog. I was still not sure about his unconditional love or loyalty. He would gurgle a slight growl at me when I insisted he find his own bed at night. He wanted to expand his territory, and the Pack, whenever he got a chance. He had pride and strength. But more than anything, he was a teacher. He did not hesitate to face whatever nature threw at him, with courage, with confidence, with vigor for life. And it could kill him in an instantaneous slam, like a high-power bullet through your gut. His teaching for us was not to push nature to its limit, not to be foolish. Not to challenge beyond our experience and ability. To wait when necessary. Could we keep him safe? He was so much a part of our Pack.

CHAPTER 19

RUNNING SHOES

After old man winter finally let go and the ice yielded to spring winds, it was a joy to get back in the waters and explore the lake.

The winter had given us time to think about and plan our future. Although we both possessed good business skills, our planning was limited to any major capital investment. Long term, we wanted to both work from the island, however, that would not pay the bills initially. We agreed that Jim would pursue carving. He had competed successfully, even been accepted into the Worlds. Now, because of no major capital investment being required, it was a good business choice to pursue. He had all the hand and power tools that most carvers would envy. As he developed his inventory for market, he could continue to upgrade our home on the island and attend to the many maintenance projects that existed. There was nothing about our old log trapper's cabin that had been built for four season comfortable living.

I was the logical choice for regular employment. Most of the jobs in the small town were seasonal from May to September, and most were in the service industry of retail or waitressing, neither of which I had done in my variety of occupations. The nearest full-time employment was 45 miles away. Find employment, learn to drive a boat, and figure out how to cross the lake daily in all seasons. We would take it one day at a time.

I was now forty and I experienced a nervousness about seeking a job. I had plenty of skill and experience, but lacked any profession marked by significant education or designation. I was a mix, no different than our rescue dog. Plenty of gumption, too qualified for entry positions, and no pedigree. I resorted to that which landed me a job when I was twenty in the big city. A rural bumpkin in the big city, I put my running shoes on. Neatly dressed for any interview, with running shoes. I had arrived in the city of Edmonton, Alberta. The wrong time. The wrong year. Engineers taking drafting job positions. The economy was in a fatal slump with oil prices slashed. Job ads were limited, line-ups of qualified professionals willing to take lesser jobs. I could barely afford rent, let alone gasoline. All those businesses were stacked within industrial blocks. I put my running shoes on.

Here I was again. There were no permanent job postings in the City of Kenora. It was more like a town, and again was influenced by the lake, seasonal, largely service industry jobs. Its population exploded in key summer months. I put my running shoes on.

"Where are you headed this afternoon?" a male voice asked.

"I have three service calls this morning, but I'm not sure what time I will get back."

I could hear two men chatting back and forth in the mezzanine above the new appliance sales area where I stood.

Their discussion continued, oblivious to me entering the store. The phone rang, and one answered.

"I'll call you from the last appointment. Do we have Rick coming in today to do some repairs?"

"Hello." I called out. I called out again. "Hello."

A head peeked over the mezzanine. "Can I help you?"

"I'm pretty sure I can help you."

They had not been looking for an employee. They just did not realize that they needed me. They ran a new appliance store, but they also repaired and did service calls. Repair was what both men knew, but they were well versed in their product. There just was not enough time in a day. I sold them on my ability to sell, my bookkeeping skills, and telephone etiquette extraordinaire. And I would learn parts. They hired me within a week, and I began the new challenge. It was not the job that was a challenge. I had never driven a boat before moving to the island. Summer was a breeze, most times.

That spring, we had traded in the sixteen-foot closed bow boat for a seventeen-foot open boat with a slightly newer motor. Marina Joe had accepted a trade-in. It seemed a fair deal to both parties, especially with our new chainsaw purchase from his store. The open boat with center console did not support a top for cover, but a slightly newer motor gave us some reassurance. If we did break down, this boat was at least equipped with oars. It was also easier to get in and out of when pulling up to rocky shorelines.

That first summer, I was blessed with calm mornings. The round trip, including boat ride, was one and a half hours and I promised an early start of seven-thirty. I knew one way across the water and was keenly aware of my route. My biggest challenge was always crossing the big water on my return. It blew from the south some eight miles, and by the time it got to my location, the waves could be in excess of three feet. I would arrive with white knuckles. Cut the wave at an angle, do not let it get you sideways. It would always be coming at me from that southerly direction, sideways. Slice it, ride it, be at one with it. And then it would hit me from the other direction as I tried to maneuver into the boathouse. Once, twice, sometimes a three-time effort to get myself lined up. Better than being lost.

I knew a bit about appliances because of my construction background, but there was still a significant learning curve. There were lots of different models in the showroom of ranges, refrigerators, dishwashers, washers and dryers and even barbecues. There were thousands of parts for do-it-yourselfers. While the owners were doing service calls, I handled the store functions. The guys were great. They were young, fun, professional, knew their business, and had integrity.

CHAPTER 20

DIFFERENT DIRECTIONS

Jim had met a couple in town when he entered a local art show. One of the artists, who was also a Board Member of the Art Council, took a liking to him. She was an accomplished flat work landscape artist. She was not only an artist, but eccentric and loveable, with a bounty of wit and humor. She had delicious one-liners. She had a round face with soft skin and happy lines around her eyes and her mouth. And she had mouth.

She was polite and appropriate for social time before dinner. Les, her husband, would do meat and drinks. She would do the rest, always ending with a rich dessert. Les would take great pains to make sure that his meat dish was lean, void of all fat and gristle. Edie believed in a deviation from calorie-wise. It was apparent in their physique. They were both close to seventy when we first met. There was not an ounce of fat on Les—sinewy would be the best description. While Edie was robust in every way. She was small-boned, with fine hands and feet, but everything else was full-bodied.

After dessert, the dishes were quickly replaced with two decks of cards to play rummy. It was each man/woman for themselves, and the competition was lively and never too serious, at least not for Edie, who took great delight in laying down first or last. There was ample time to have discussions about politics, the lake, art, philosophies of life, and the dog down the street whom they'd recently adopted via daily feeding.

"Oh yes, I do remember the days when we lived on our island. I was frightened out of my wits half the time," Edie recalled.

"I can't imagine you ever being frightened out of your wits." I giggled at the thought.

"Oh, I was. I had three children. I was terrified that they would fall in the water. I made little harnesses for them, tied them to trees so that they could wander around, but never reach the lake."

"You're kidding?"

"I'll take that card." Les was taking advantage of a card Edie laid down.

"Les. That's just not fair." Edie went on with her story. "I had chores, and dinner, and on an island to boot. I had to tie those little devils for fear that they would just head off to town. Remember, our island was close to mainland. We could practically see people blow their noses." She paused. "I think I have rummy."

And so it was, she laid her cards down once again.

We shared stories. Kindred spirits in different life times. By late summer, they introduced their plans to go to Portugal. Les was learning Spanish and Edie wanted to paint their colors. They had a two-car garage with Edie's studio and a one-bedroom apartment up top. If we wanted to stay there the winter, we could. They needed someone to cat sit while they were gone. We would close the island, just like every other person on the lake did, and I could keep my job in Kenora. There would be no ice roads to build, no firewood to cut or buy, and perhaps we could save a bit. Although the apartment/studio was heated with a wood burning stove in the garage, Les had all the winter wood cut and stacked. It was a win/win for all of us—except Sekima.

Being cooped up in a small apartment for the winter was not exactly the adventure we sought; however, it was a blessing financially. Jim was able to carve and paint in Edie's studio without endless hours of island chores. He was able to book some shows, and we had time to observe the market, and the challenge of marketing his carvings. His past was largely competition. Hundreds of hours on a piece for a competition was necessary, but not something the market would bare in local art and craft shows.

We had a few television channels on a small set that Edie and Les had provided. The dark, long winter nights gave us ample time to discuss how Jim could maintain the quality that he was accustomed to while reducing the hours on each individual piece. Our discussions went from relief carvings to half birds, to no detailing at all. One day while Jim was feeding the fire, he observed several birch pieces thrown off to the side, as they would not maintain the perfect balance for a woodpile. They were irregular shapes and thicknesses, about the size of a barstool seat. By the time I got home, he had carved an eagle's head and a good portion of its upper body on a birch piece.

Like oak trees, birch is notorious for dropping off large branches, leaving the bark or skin with scars, and the inner layers of wood with twisted fibers of healing. It was with these twisted shapes that he found the image that spoke to him. The eagle was a relief carving becoming a coffee table piece that we explored as yet another dimension of his carving. Its large head and prominent beak, its amber eye seemed to follow us around the room, the eagle's presence symbolic.

The previous winter had not only humbled us to nature's challenges, but created a tranquility amidst the obstacles; we were now being led on another path of transformation. We were given the opportunity to not only be nothing, but based on our previous lifestyle, we were doing nothing. Our creativity blossomed and flourished. As the deep of winter slipped by, so did the snow, evaporating and receding like a slow-moving tide. On weekends, we would ski to the island in early morning, spend the day dreaming, and be back on mainland before dark.

It was on one of those trips that we found yet another appealing concept for Jim's carvings. As most things did for us, it came directly from the spirit of the lake. At first it was just some leftover boathouse barnboard that had been left heaped in a pile for further potential use. We explored the idea of placing a half bird on the face of the wood. Although barnboard had not yet become the "in thing," it had a draw for cottage décor, which was definitely our market. What it lacked was any artistic dimension of form. It did take care of quality. If Jim could carve less of a bird, it was less time, without losing the detail that was so much of his expression and mastery of each piece.

Our winter was over. We had not been lulled to sleep. We had drifted to a place of wondering, experimenting with ideas, dreaming in different directions, waiting for seeds to sprout. I had secured a full-time position at a local fishing resort that would start in mid-May. As much as I loved working with the guys that owned the service and appliance business, I had been spending half my earned dollars on gas and driving time. Spring had arrived.

CHAPTER 21

DONALD NUTT

The local fishing resort was right outside the little community on mainland, and offered full-time employment in a bookkeeping position. I wished that I could have continued working for the guys. The guys were easygoing and appreciative; they demonstrated good character and morals. They were not sexist, and they showed respect for anyone they came across.

Then there was the resort owner. I had heard some good, but mostly bad. There was such a contrast between the two employers. I remember my introduction to him, sitting across from him in his office. He was a big man. He appeared to belong to his oversized executive desk. He was not proportioned properly for a big man. There were certain features about him that were appealing, like his large, compelling eyes with abundant eyelashes. It stopped there. His face fell away to a weak mouth and chin that was best kept in the shadows. He had orange/red thinning hair pushed from the far-left side to the right side, as though he was attempting to hide something in the middle. He appeared to have depth to his chest under his tightly knit logo shirt, but it did not belong to his shoulders, which slid off his neck at a severe angle. Weak shoulders as though he had been carrying heavy burdens.

I had my mind set. For all the nasty rumors I had heard about the divorced man and his family company, I wanted this job under the terms Jim had coached and re-coached me on. It was definitely Jim's strength. My terms were simple. A $2200 monthly salary for a Monday to Friday accounting position, with a $300 per month raise at the end of three months. We also needed a place to live at the lodge during the lake freeze-up and break-up, if we chose. They had plenty of cabins, and it was an option for maintaining full-time employment.

"We are the biggest and best resort in all of this region. Just take a look around. How could you ever beat this scenery?" He puffed up his chest.

"It is grand. We moved here for the beauty and remoteness." I knew a bit about stroking egos.

He explained that his dad had bought the resort. His dad had taken ill and he'd had to take over. He had no experience, but he considered himself brilliant. He was modeling himself after Walt Disney.

"What experience have you determined is necessary for the position?" I tried to scope out the job requirements and lead him towards defining what contribution I would make. The ad they had placed was vague.

"We want personality here. Someone that will be part of the family." He had introduced me to his assistant, and he now included her in the discussion. "Isn't that right, Carlie?"

I wasn't sure why Carlie was in the interview. She had not been included up until now. I had been led to believe that she was the Office Manager, his personal assistant, but she had not taken any notes. I knew she had some importance to him.

"Of course, Don. That's what we are here—a family." She looked pensive and uncomfortable, and her eyes were riveted on Donald.

Hmm, no skills required. It was obvious that they had not assessed the position and probably had no idea what was really happening in the department. I cut straight to the chase, outlining my skills and what wage I expected. I noticed a slight surprise at my wage request, but no noticeable reaction came until I mentioned my expectation to work Monday to Friday. I had heard that all staff worked six days a week.

"We moved here from the city to enjoy life in this beautiful paradise," I emphasized. "That means a regular five-day work week. I put plenty of hours in when I had my own company, and that's not my focus right now."

I had Carlie in my peripheral vision and noticed her jaw stiffen. She glared at Donald. She had not once looked at me, nor made any comments. That scowl towards her boss did not indicate a normal boss/employee relationship. I suddenly got it. Not why she was so upset, but that Carlie was intimate with Donald. There was an unspoken dance between them. I had ignored her during the interview and now immediately felt regret. I tried to make a quick adjustment. "Carlie, how do you feel about that? Do you anticipate any difficulties?" There was no point in letting Carlie make her case behind closed doors.

Carlie ignored the question and directed her view towards Donald, who had suddenly pushed his swivel chair back, prepared for the rebuttal. "You know it won't work, Don. There's too much happens here seven days a week. I can hardly take one day off. If you're asking me, no, it won't work."

Donald looked at me, slightly turning his palms up in the air, rapidly moved from the solidness of his big oak desk. "There you have it." He spoke pleadingly with a slight whine to his voice as though she had stripped him of his manliness. "The girl that is currently in the position is barely able to keep afloat in six days. When she does payroll, she's in her office until midnight. I have to go with Carlie on this one. It's probably not possible."

The mere knowledge of how they interviewed gave me a good idea of the inefficiencies that must be taking place on a daily basis.

I was not willing to give up my position so easily. "Okay, I'll tell you what. I'm confident that I can do the job in five days, not six as you suggest. I will not only eliminate the inefficiencies, but I'll be able to provide you with better financial reporting and improve your purchasing methods." I was thinking they probably had no purchasing policies. "Of course, if I have to be here to get the work done, then I'll stay, no questions asked."

"See, Carlie, she'll guarantee that the work gets done." He looked like he was begging, his eyes wide and innocent.

I gave Donald my biggest smile of confidence and assurance. I was certain that he rarely saw competency in his operation fraught with a small local pool and largely transient seasonal employees. I hoped that he recognized that I had more skills than he had seen in a very long time. He had to work on the mistress; he was trying his best to have both ways. I still was not sure how much control Carlie had on his decisions.

"Don, you just don't get it. There's cash that comes in every day of the week. Sunday is our biggest check-out day of the week. I'm here from six to seven on the weekends." Carlie looked agitated, fuming under that hardened exterior. Carlie was evidently working her ass off for this guy in more ways than one. I empathized with her but knew from experience that her path was the wrong one. I did not imagine he would ever tell anyone that he loved her, nor would he ever introduce her as anything other than his Office Manager.

"The banks aren't open on the weekend anyways, Carlie, and Monday I would be here to ensure that it was reconciled and deposited."

I was only too familiar with Carlie's dilemma. Many years prior I had been like Carlie—the mistress. I had thought I was in love. I had thought we were a team. He had not loved me, and all his promises to make me a partner had been lies. It took me a long time to realize that. Too long; too many years of my life trying to understand love that had been twisted and strangled from me in my youth. He thanked me for making him his first million. I was so proud. And yet, I was never good enough to show off to his friends, never good enough to introduce as a girlfriend. Good enough to bring home to Mom and Pop's place as the girl that he employed, but never good enough to be that *one*. Good enough to party with, to dance with, to screw, but never good enough to be that *one*. Always empty promises when I tried to walk away. And then finally I found the courage to walk away, even though I had waited too long.

I was sure that Carlie fought many such battles, and I was even more certain that Carlie won only the battles that never mattered to Donald in the first place. This was not one of them. There was no amount of reason or hostility that Carlie could demonstrate that would change his mind. He wanted me as an employee. He recognized an asset when he saw it. He always got what he wanted. The more someone stood in the way, the more he would double down. He pretended that her opinion mattered. It did not. Even the opinion of his children that claimed their right to the business would not have mattered. They would always pretend they had authority or the power to sway him. They never did. They never could.

I knew it all too well. It was a critical part of his personality that I immediately recognized and was wary of. At what lengths would he go if he wanted something? What would he do to someone or something that stood in his way? I knew I could do very little for Carlie, very little for others that he might manipulate and abuse. When you finally really get the personality of the narcissist and understand that your position is inferior to theirs, you need to keep your head down so they do not notice you. They are too busy in self-absorption to notice you, anyway. They are always the most dangerous when nothing appears to be happening that's about them. They cannot tolerate not being in the limelight. They will create an inferno that only they can put out to become the hero they wished they could be, and never would. I would keep my head down. I had to. Our livelihood depended on it. I knew there would be many he used and discarded. I knew he would want something from me someday that I likely would not provide. I did not know what. I did not know when. I just knew it would happen.

CHAPTER 22

GOING HOME

We could not leave our little apartment too soon. Edie and Les were home. They were happy to be back, shared stories, and we had no hurry by their measure to leave. I worked every day, Monday to Friday. If we left too soon during the week, we would be trapped in break-up. So, we waited, but were anxious to return home to our island. Everyone had left the lake—all regular vehicles including snow machines, all ATVs. The ice was in its final stages, black, white, black. We anticipated that if I had Friday off, we could make an early ski out to the island, and by Monday we would be boating out. We'd be taking a chance, but our island called us. We had seen the first black ice, the crystal white, and now it was a mix of both. There was no ice left at the landing for any vehicle, but there was still over a foot or two of ice off another shore facing north and west. It led us to believe that we could make it, and there would be plenty of ice around our island.

We chose the last weekend before we would be able to boat to our island. We had already arranged to have the marina bring our boat out on Sunday, or Monday if there were too many ice flows.

There were already many shallower bays that were open. Lobstick Bay where Edie and Les lived was already wide open. Regina and Long Bay were traversable. It was only the deepest part of the lake, Whitefish, where we lived, that held fast, but even much of the ice in the inlets had receded.

Perhaps we should have left earlier in the morning, before dawn, while temperatures still hovered at freezing. It was not easy to break away from the breakfast Edie and Les had prepared, the last goodbyes, as we both knew our daily exchanges were ending. By the time we got to the landing it was well after eleven a.m. The spring sun was brilliant and the ice glistened.

Spring stimulates the senses. The cool moistness of the air widening your nostrils—versus the stunning shrinking inwards to evade the dry frigid winter air. There is an opening, an awareness, a blossoming rather than shrinking inwardly to spare reserves.

Sekima took off at a fast pace. We let him loose less than fifty feet from shore. The ice conditions were not suitable for tiny hooves of deer or moose who would fall on the slippery surface, and likewise no predators would be interested in travelling.

There had been enough melting and re-freezing to prepare a near-skating condition. We were having trouble maneuvering our long cross-country skis. We had no grip on the smooth surface. As we got out further into the wide expanse, a southerly wind chose to make our travel more difficult. The idea of wearing skis was simple—it would be faster, and a more even distribution of weight over weakening ice. But it was becoming a struggle. The conditions were worsening, a glistening water film on the top, and a southerly wind that was strong enough to push us back for every foot that we took forward. At this pace, we would be hard pressed to make it to the island by dusk. We were making very slow progress. Certainly, it would be faster walking.

We were not a third of the way. We were struggling. We were determined to finally go home. Jim was bitter with the progress on the skis. He finally decided to remove his skis and walk. It provided momentary relief.

Jim was ahead of me, at least fifteen feet. It was unexpected. We were focused on our challenges at making progress, and now suddenly we had danger. The step, I remember it so well. One step in life in the wrong direction can change the rest of life as we know it.

I saw his right leg disappear to the knee. The ice caved under his weight. Splinters flew upwards. Jagged shards of ice over a foot long, slivers of rotting crystal. Like birth and death, they were returning to their original formation of water. Under Jim's weight as he shifted from one leg to the other, the pressure had been too much.

His instincts were spot on. He went spread eagle to distribute his weight. He pushed off with the one remaining leg that remained on solid ice—or at least ice that had not given way. He landed several feet from the open hole. Black water bubbled up and took the place of where his leg had been. I stood stunned.

Jim had dropped his skis on impact when he hit the ice. They slid five feet away from him, driven by the force of his fall. He crawled first to the skis and put them on lying down.

He finally spoke. "Don't come close. Stay away."

"I'm just going to get your poles to you so you can get up." I was nervous. I did not want to move closer but he needed some leverage to get up without putting excessive weight on any one limb.

The poles had slid the furthest away and I recovered them for him, sliding them towards him on the slippery ice. He struggled to get up, his skis sliding this way and that. Using the strength of his arms, grappling with the poles mid-way up on the shaft to use their metal points for stability, he was finally up. His skis had crossed and he stood precariously trying to maintain his balance. Skis finally unlocked, he propelled himself forward to give distance between himself and the gaping hole.

Sekima was far ahead of us now, picking up all the smells of spring. The south wind was gusting, spreading familiar scents of home and beyond. We recovered. Our heartbeats slowed. Nature, in all its beauty, spread its wings before us. The smells, the glorious calling of spring on the lake that no one in their right mind can resist. The reason that every cabin owner hurries to open, like they're driven by the calling of migratory birds. Nature calls all of us, deep within us, the calling to come home.

She lay before us. The sky, its brilliant blue with slight wisps of cloud trail. The reckless pattern of pine, of red, of white, of spruce, of jacks that occupied the shorelines, tightly knit friends, with silvery white birch and speckled poplar, just to tantalize the senses. The ice spread before us, resisting no more, in her final months of pregnancy. The waters below preserved and cured by the months of sleep. The smell of spring.

We crossed the remainder of Whitefish with our skis on. There it was in the distance—our home. It was the island. She lay beyond the reef marker. The sun sat low. A rusty orange, with pink flavor, like a tropical drink. Sekima raced from the shore to great us, as if to say, "Come on, there's no worry, all is well here." Full-coat Alaskan malamute, delirious and exuberant.

We would spend the next hours getting the cabin up to a reasonable temperature to survive the night. She was locked into winter. We would start the PIG, and the big heater. We would start coal oil lanterns. We would shovel our way to the outhouse, where mounds of snow stayed hidden from the rays of the sun. We would thank the universe and God that we were all safe, and tomorrow we would deal with other utilities. For tonight, we were home.

CHAPTER 23

COLD DIP

Jim could not spend every day on the island. Occasionally, he and Sekima would head out for the day to pick up something from the lumber yard that was needed for a project. He would drop me off at the public dock and head out. It was not often, only as our money permitted. On his return to the island, he would sometimes stop to explore an area of public land that might be of interest for us when I was off on a weekend.

We had always passed an indented cove on the backside of one of the islands that had some interesting rock cuts and tree formations. Jim decided to take a look. He watched the shoreline warily for rocks, especially when he did not have me as his scout, sitting on the bow. He also watched warily for black bear that could be trouble in the spring, with cubs in tow. He shut the engine off as the boat nudged a new shore. He told Sekima to stay. He steadied himself with the bow of the boat and stepped onto a ledge of shale. The shale was slick with algae, as it usually is when the shallows of water move back and forth over the surface. It could be as slippery as walking on glare ice. And then it happened.

I slapped the pine table and laughed as he told me.

"He bolted. I couldn't do a thing. I couldn't hold on. All I had was one hand on the metal tip of the bow."

"You lost the boat?" I imagined it slipping from the shore into the cold water.

"He jumped. One big bound, using all the muscles he had in his hind legs to push the boat away, and here I am grabbing the tip of the boat and a piece of slimy shale so I wouldn't fall."

"Oh no! But you managed to hang on to the boat?" My laughter dissipated in the air.

"No. Of course not." He seemed a bit disappointed that I would have thought he could have recovered his balance and the boat in a moment's notice.

He explained that the westerly wind swept the boat sidewise. Sekima ran up the bank; Jim thought he must have been after a bear.

"So, what did you do?"

"The obvious. I jumped into ice cold water to get to the boat before it got away on us."

I wondered if I would have been triggered to go after Sekima, protect him first. Foolishly of course.

"My clothes were soaking wet. I had to take them off."

"Oh! You have to be still cold." I now had the full realization of what had occurred. The waters were too cold for swimming. It could not be much above fifty degrees in early spring. This was not the same as swimming during our late September days. The ice flows had barely melted out in the big waters.

I had just started my job as the Account Manager of the resort. My days were spent attempting to streamline a resort with archaic accounting procedures, no human resource policies, and severe cultural issues. Let me put it this way: the resort was adapting from days when guests were greeted with bottles of whiskey and anything goes with female staff. Maybe the girls got paid, maybe they did not. She would be some parent's young daughter on a summer job.

I was attempting to understand and deal with a family and business of nepotism—an operations manager that was sleeping with the boss, and a boss owner that was a dry drunk. He had already shown himself to be a predator. He was going out of his way to create trouble between staff members, would have temper tantrums that turned his thin skin blazing red. He would throw his leather bomber jacket on the floor, stomp off, slamming his office door. Shortly after, Carlie would be beckoned to his office.

I understood how Jim felt, plunged into cold water, no choice. I felt like jumping ship already, but in a town of 250 people, and very limited full-time jobs, I was destined to suck it up. I would likely have to rely on some business and life experiences that I did not really want to relive. Donald was not unfamiliar to me.

Somehow our past never quite leaves us. Cut down a spider web with your broom or duster, only to find that the web appears again a short time later. It has its favorite hanging-out place, resilient, persevering. Although it looks like fine threads, it is embedded, fairly secure in its foundation. In eastern religions, it might be called karma. There is *déjà vu* from the French. There are psychological, philosophical, and religious deliberations as to why we create anew the same shit that we left behind.

I had one strand of that spider web floating around. I feared that if I let my guard down, my past vulnerabilities would be exposed, that somehow that web would find crevices to rebuild. Donald was repulsive to me. I felt strong enough, because of Jim, and because of what I had gone through in my life, to isolate myself from any emotional damage. But could I look away while he was doing it to others? It was always a dilemma for me. Many times in the past, I could not recognize personal and emotional abuse. I was now experiencing the same through others. Were they being abused? Were they willing and able? There was something very sick about him. I did not have to be there months or years to recognize the signs.

I had made myself a promise that I would keep my head down, but there were days when I could not help but reach out. Carlie would be the most difficult to help. She did not know she needed help. He would intimidate her, say hurtful things that made her feel she had done something wrong, make up and start all over.

There were times I could feel her pain. I wanted to look away, but there was some crazy motivation that I had to fight those in authoritative positions that took advantage of people. It was not to better myself. It often had ways of weakening me. I would feel incredibly alone and in pain because the very people that I tried to protect from being victimized did not know they were suffering. It took me years of self-improvement to become strong enough to defend myself from predators. Here I was, knowing I had the defenses, but fine fiber webs wanted to form, carefully designed to show me my own life in a mirror. Why?

"You're home. You're safe," I said to Jim. I imagined cold water splashing lightly on my face, and I felt the sudden relief of coming to a safe home, to my family, the Pack. The big malamute had his eyes scrunched closed, blocking us out as he digested his supper. The rich smells of spring wafted through our windows, and the lake rippled quietly. The day had ended with new lessons to be learned. Sekima would be taught to stay in the boat until told to get out. And I would be constantly trying to pluck any thread so that it could never re-attach.

Jim looked knowingly at me, placing his big hand on top of mine. "Looks like your day was like mine."

"He's such an awful person." I scrunched my eyes, trying to erase his face. "I'm trying really hard."

"If you need, I'll speak to him. I don't want to see you like this. Every day it seems there's something else."

"No. It would make things worse. I can do this."

Jim got up from the table, crossing to my side. "I'm still cold."

I stood up. Almost a foot taller than I, he took me in his arms, swaying gentling back and forth. My body yielded to the gentle rhythm between us. We stood like that for a very long time before he led me to our bed. His body felt cool against mine. He kissed me all over until I thought I would explode. Our bodies became entwined. Our passion peaked and fell away. The day was left behind as quickly as a cold dip.

CHAPTER 24

NEIGHBORS

I took my fair share of scares over the summer. Summer winds always brought huge waves across Whitefish, and I was still a novice with a boat. I had just learned how to drive a boat, at forty—*yikes*. I hated the winds that started on the far south of Whitefish Bay; by the time they got to our shores, the waves could be two-to-three-foot rollers. I had to cross them at an angle. I could not parallel the waves or I would swamp. They were not really waves, as most people think of them. They were rollers, slow moving crescent moons. They had accumulated strength over many hours, like an intense hurricane building forces for many days over the warming ocean. Those times were tense. White knuckles.

We had met some of the island owners, largely from the United States, that had taken on small cottage life, relatively inexpensive and expansively beautiful in the 50s and 60s. The properties had low taxes, and these cottagers enjoyed the beauty of something north of the border. They were mostly educators who could take the summer off, and in some cases, they had a long history and relationship with the glories of hunting and fishing in the wild.

That summer I wore one of Jim's old long sleeve shirts with the arms cut off, the tails long enough so that I wore nothing beneath. I worked outside, digging up the ground in hopes of finding suitable soil for a garden. I felt connected to the earth once more, as I had when I was first placed in the garden to play while my mother worked the soil.

I heard the boat come off step and someone yell "Hello!"

I scurried back to the cabin to quickly throw on shorts and scrambled down to the dock to meet whoever had pulled up. Jim was disinterested. He had no desire or inclination to welcome anyone to our island who had come unannounced. Though announcing oneself was not an option when you did not have a phone.

"Hi," I said breathlessly, with Sekima by my side.

"Oh, hello. We thought we would drop by and introduce ourselves. I'm Bernadette and this is my husband, George." Bernadette smiled a warm broad smile, bright blue eyes shining. She was girlish looking with her short curly blonde hair and pale skin, soft and unblemished.

I guessed these were our island neighbors, at least in the summer months. It did not seem the time to meet anyone, especially with all this work that we had to do. The interruption spoiled my daydream that I was here with my lover on a remote island, my slight ass feeling the kiss of wind.

"I'm Connie, Jim is somewhere. Pleased to meet you."

"You bought the place recently. We didn't know the Van Horts very well. We have an island property just over there." Bernadette pointed in a westerly direction. Bells and whistles went off as I remembered that November day when the boat barely got us home. There was a cluster of cabins that certainly looked tempting for refuge. Further introductions were made. Where are you from? How long you been here? I assumed this was all basic stuff to figure out whether they considered us acceptable island neighbors, or they were just being nosy as people are.

"Well, we are having a few people over this Saturday night and thought you might want to meet some of your island neighbors. Nothing fancy." Bernadette was definitely the outgoing type. Her husband appeared friendly enough, but it was Bernadette doing the social nuisances. She was likely around Jim's age, early fifties. Having seen no neighbor offer friendship since we had arrived, my social nature overcame any dream of an isolated island with my lover.

"Let me talk to Jim. It sounds wonderful. What could I bring?"

And so, we took the short boat ride over and were introduced to five other couples that had islands, or were visiting.

People were inquisitive as to who would be spending winters on an island in the Canadian north. I had not realized that I was an anomaly until after it was explained to me what was expected. It was expected that I would be ugly, heavily built, and likely Indigenous. This was the expectation of what a woman would have to look like, be like, in order to live on an island year-round through the brutal Canadian winters, without the familiar comforts of a typical home. They wondered how I bathed, how I could do without an indoor bath, did I miss the arts or theatre. Endless questions that brought our differences in stark contrast. I knew I was discussed before, during, and after I left the party.

Later that night, I tried to rid myself of thoughts of not belonging. I rationalized that that was not the case, but it stuck with me that I was different, and that difference meant I did not fit in.

Some of it was connected to my upbringing. As the youngest of four with over five years difference, I spent most of my younger years trying to fit in. I was the baby to them. It seemed like I was always running to keep up, to be like them. There was too big a gap and the differences were too obvious. As much as I tried through my school years to be friendly and outgoing with peers, the more I tried, the more I drew attention to the differences. Part of it may have been how rural we lived compared to many of my classmates. I rode a horse. They rode a bicycle. My extra-curriculum was a bus ride home, there's basketball and track. But a larger part was my way of thinking. It was like I grew up too fast, with a mind that questioned everything in early days of high school - our existence as human beings, the essence of love and friendship, what I would be when I grew up. I felt a deep sadness to be so strange to others, and yet I seemed to create it wherever I went.

My lifestyle was now setting me apart. I tried to imagine other people in the world that struggled to fit in. There were plenty of them. Many of them became my closest friends. Many of them I left in the city, and I wondered whether I would ever see them again. Our very differences were what kept us together. Never far apart in spirit.

I was both nostalgic and hopeful. I hoped that the people on neighboring islands had a special relationship with nature. I hoped that we had at least that one thing in common, people that wanted to protect these pristine waters. It would make it okay to be different in other ways.

And so that is how our island relationships began. People who had a connection, a very long enduring connection to a body of water that everyone loved. The lake had a way of bringing people together. Its beauty, its Windigo spirit that beckoned. For many of us, it was the only thing we had in common. That is what we belonged to.

CHAPTER 25

TRAPPED

I remembered Lilly, the person who I replaced at the resort. She certainly did not fit in. Many employees there came because they did not fit in elsewhere. They sought new beginnings, hoping to make new friends and rid themselves of something they left behind. Many were barely out of high school, now away from their peers and parents, striving to fit in amidst others that had no connection to their lives or location. Some were older, feeling that life would hold new beginnings in a different location. The owner did not really fit in with the community, so he built his own, hoping to isolate himself from people that might criticize him. He made his right-hand person, Carlie—who was persuasive and caring to wayward souls—the congenial keeper of his twisted ways.

I recognized Carlie's entrapment, the webs that surrounded her. She thought she had power. She had none. She thought he loved her. He loved himself much more. He had her for various reasons. Having her for sex was one reason. The other was simple. She was loyal. When he did incomprehensible, bizarre, and often cruel things to employees, she was there to distort the truth. *He's under so much pressure, he didn't mean it that way, he's really looking after everyone, he's so misunderstood.* She made a great press secretary for him. She lied for him. I was already aware that she treated staff as though they were her own children and I wondered how difficult it must be for her to sleep some nights.

Lilly had elected to stay for three weeks of my training, and for days on end I was obliged to sort through reams of paper. Lilly was wrinkled and tiny—hardly old enough to be that wrinkled. The accounting office was scarcely bigger than a small bathroom, barely bigger than Donald's desk. I sat so close to Lilly I could count the wrinkles on her neck. The space was hardly big enough for a desk and chair, let alone the historical data for an operation of this size. What became apparent very quickly was how the resort was being run by emotional impulse, mismanaged at many levels, and successful primarily because of the abundance of free resources, the lake and fish.

I remember those early days so vividly.

The operation had 100 to 150 seasonal employees, and their historical data had been printed to become alphabetically kept, rather than relying on computer back-ups. The mere fact that there were back-ups in the safe, and that these people were as gone as dandelion seeds, did not seem to matter. There was redundancy, and it was easy for me to see how I could become a significant asset for the company.

The reason that Lilly was leaving was that she had met her sugar daddy at the lodge. He lived somewhere in the mid-west and Lilly was moving, lock, stock, and barrel. There was no job opportunity for her as she would not be able to acquire an American visa for some time. For this reason, she was compelled to hang on to her current position and celebrate her accomplishments. She treated me as though I was fresh out of high school, but she had an axe to grind with a few of the staff and felt it important to share her thoughts. To her there was more than one bully, and more than one oppressor.

"Never cross the Queen." She reeked of cigarettes and perfume.

"What will happen?" I inquired, suspecting who the Queen might be.

"She'll have your ass. She plays Donald. Leads him around by his crotch, this way and that." She dangled a wrinkled finger back and forth across her keyboard.

"The witch, his ex-wife, Janet, use to be real bad, but she left a few years back. Got caught spanking one of the guests. It was divorce after a few times like that." She had paused, settling the mouse cursor over a payment she wished to make. "Always make sure these checks that I'm printing have signatures on them when they come back from the Queen. She'll miss the odd one, and heavens, you'll never hear the end of it when it gets returned. It will be your fault. Like I have the time." She vibrated her head, as though shaking whatever ugliness had followed that thought.

"I'll make sure when I put them in the envelopes." I couldn't fathom how Carlie would miss signing a check, let alone Lilly missing that it hadn't been signed. "So, Carlie's the Queen?"

Lilly turned her head as though alarmed. She rolled her eyes. "Of course, you hadn't noticed?" Without waiting for a response, she continued. "Carlie saw her opportunity when Janet got caught. What's good for the goose is good for the gander. Story goes that he was giving her a drive home after working late one night and they didn't make it a mile from here. Stopped for a quickie."

"You're kidding. That's crazy. Who caught them?" I had seen the signs from day one.

"My ex-boyfriend, Dan, that's who."

I had tried to control my surprise. Lilly was dumping her boyfriend and moving up in the world. From what I had already experienced with Dan, he was a kind soul, but an alcoholic, who may or may not show up for work. It took me a while to realize that Donald kept him that way. So long as Dan was dependent, he was also incredibly loyal.

Lilly no longer needed the resort drunk and was now making her way with a mid-west high roller who loved fishing in Canada.

"I know it's true, but Carlie doesn't know I know. She lets on like nothing is happening. But everybody knows." She placed heavy emphasis on the *everybody*.

There were people of different color, gender, and ability. There were fractures in personalities, likely scars from upbringing, or just life itself. My scars probably were not much different than theirs. At twenty years old, I checked in with my first psychologist. I was broken. Most psychologists wanted me to remember that day, dragged me through every moment, every feeling, until I could not cry any longer. It was not that I could not remember. It was not that I could not tell you who it was, when it happened, that second time. It was plain and simple—sexual assault. I just could not remember the first time. I was too young, or perhaps my defenses would not let me remember. I could only remember the pretty dress and running, and I knew in my heart that it was him, and what I was running from.

After three psychologists and many years, I called it quits. I was still broken, and my world changed, but likely not in the way anyone would imagine. I called it quits because I finally was mad enough at the professionals for dragging me through painful memories, like somehow, I would forgive and heal and my world would be a better place. But it was not working. I had decided not to forgive a long time ago. I was not angry at that uncle. I no longer even cared who he was, or how he was. I was simply tormented by what had happened.

Encounters with men were primarily for sex. Partners that I had cared about brought back memories that were hardwired to a part of me, a part of my brain, screaming. They were not visual, they were only words, *I hate you, I hate you.* A person that I had loved had blemished me for life. Love and sex all mixed up, like one of those cakes that blend chocolate and white, the edges had lost their perfect lines, became blurred and fuzzy. I needed to keep them separate. I desperately kept love in a box so it wouldn't be tainted by sex.

I would have intercourse with someone I cared about and drift away in my mind to a better place so that my body could feel the pleasure of my sexuality. The moment that I wanted to truly connect with that person with all parts of me, I was led back to a place that was painful and sick. Keep them separate or feel the pain.

I healed a lot. Some scar tissue still remained, like the callous that never quite leaves the fingers of a guitar player. I'd taught myself how to overcome the hateful voices. And I'd vowed never to force myself to be intimate with anyone unless my head space was clear, unless I could be at one with myself. I had viewed myself as broken, and after a while it did not matter anymore. I accepted the bandages that I had placed over those parts of myself, that protected me. I accepted myself just the way I was and stopped trying to be someone else. I am grateful that Jim accepted me too.

We all have scars. We are not unique in that way. Our stories might be slightly different. Perhaps some of these differences are even recognizable on the outside, but I was pretty sure that there was little difference on the inside. We all wanted to be accepted for who we were. In many ways, we all wanted to fit in. But most of all, we wanted to accept ourselves. Some find it. Some don't.

The resort provided housing for the seasonal staff; relationships were forged as people worked and lived together, all of them trying to fit in. They were trapped together. For a brief period of time, they were forced to become part of the culture that existed. They would adapt, or go home. For me, I worked and went home. It was not intentional, but I was separated from them, by the lake, by the island. Again, it seemed I was blessed by nature.

CHAPTER 26

SUMMER PROGRESS

Summer life on the island was easy. Diving into the cool blue waters off the dock, where Paul had brought the wood up. We had never finished the exterior of the cabin. It was insulated with sheets of white solid polystyrene held primitively together with boards from the old boathouse that we had dismantled.

Part of Jim's development of his company was engineering of a product, like stucco, a grey polymer that adhered to a skin like membrane, rather than the traditional metal wire. It became the main summer project—that and storm windows to provide a double pane affect to the flimsy single pane summer windows. They were mostly the very old style eight-by-ten-inch glass panels set inside wooden grilles.

To enhance the aesthetics of the exterior, we found a local mill that had slabs for cheap. They were the outside round of a red pine with the bark left on. They became a trim affect to the bottom of the cabin, rough-cut, wide-trim boards accented the windows, and a twelve-inch rough-cut fascia gave the place a Frank Lloyd Wright architecture in the woods. It was all very basic with what limited money we had. With both our backgrounds in construction, the place evolved simply, and over time.

I had good friends visit from the west. After they left, I knew I would likely never see them again. It was just too far and we were too remote. I cried inside. It was a choice I had made to leave, and with it I accepted my significant losses. I prepared myself instead to include those around me in my life fold. I had moved in order to reclaim a part of my past, a pioneering life, like my parents had, without children, of course, and hopefully without their poverty.

Good parents never let on that they are struggling. Mine certainly did not. They had children and they had pride. In my parents' case, because we had a small farm and my father could usually sustain full time employment, we were far better off than many.

I am not sure those same truths are for everyone. Sometimes, parents just cannot make it. They get lost. I realized a long time ago that my parents did the best they could with what little they had. They did not bemoan their struggles, but somehow, I knew they struggled, because the last thing I wanted was their life. I did not want to relive being poor. Remembering the pile of us in one bed, the little log cabin with single pane windows, no indoor water, the trips to the outhouse in the winter. I thought that was pretty normal then. But I was born in 1957, when indoor water and baths were pretty routine for most of North America. So, when I got older, I realized there was something slightly different about how I had grown up. I wanted those pioneer days, but not with the struggles that existed for them, not their worries and hardships. We were not poor in the sense that we were deprived of food and shelter, but there was no extra money for anything. There was no money for the school cafeteria. There was no funding for extra-curricular in our schools. There was no money for extended education. All colleges and universities were long distances. There was no support for tuition, and minimal help for an apartment, furniture, or basic needs when I went to college. I did get a single bed, bought by my parents from a second-hand store. I remember it. It had a soft worn mattress and a pretty blue headboard. Cardboard boxes made good lamp and end tables; I even had a larger one for a coffee table. I was on my own. I made my own way at seventeen. There were bad times and good times. There was no one there to guide me, so I slipped and fell many times, blindly unaware of the pitfalls of life. It took years of exploration, of dedication to wellness, of persistence, to heal the hurt. My parents didn't touch me with a "poor me" attitude. They touched me with heart and soul to respect the life I had. I grew up with gratitude, the biggest blessing that was passed on. I was compelled to recreate that basic, natural life, recapture those simple values. City culture had been devouring me. No one knew better than me. I had felt that internal sadness that comes from losing a part of yourself along the way. I was done with the bad relationships with men. I was done with making it up the ladder. I was done with emptiness and meaninglessness. I had achieved a lot, and had suddenly felt a plateau that was uncomfortable. I desperately needed something beyond my successes and achievements. I needed to feel at home.

The painful losses of those friends from my past were acknowledged and let go. The comfort of their love and acceptance was replaced with a peacefulness of knowing I had returned home to nature. By doing that, I had returned home to the biggest part of me. It was a different time, and new friends would be made. We even managed to throw a summer party, inviting the island people that we had met, and Paul with his girlfriend. Everyone brought their own lawn chairs, and we sat around lopsided on the uneven ground. I cannot recall what we ate. Everyone brought a dish, and as you probably know, potlucks are usually pretty good.

I was getting beyond trying to fit in. There emerged an acceptance on my part that it can take a long time for friendships to get good, like sharp cheddar cheese or aged Scotch. It was going to take a while. Perhaps it would never be. There was a faint internal whisper. I could wait.

That first year, my kitchen had a total of about four feet of working countertop, some of it sink. But like the seeming hardship of an outdoor toilet, when you are truly nurturing your soul, there is really no hardship at all. They say that having gratitude is a big step to being happy. I say that if you embrace the little things in life with gratitude, you will likely be able to face the big things that might otherwise break you. Maybe you will even find internal peace.

CHAPTER 27

DISCOVERY

Temperatures in the Canadian North are relatively cool in the summer. Our highest temperatures did not exceed 86 to 90°F, and that would likely only last a week or two in mid-summer. We explored the lake as much as possible, as summers were short. We fished, we swam, we studied the unique aspects of the lake and nature. There were remnants of Prisoner of War Camps from World War II. There were pictographs. There was history of Indian raiding parties.

Although we had come up with a few ideas for Jim's carvings that would reduce the time he spent on them—and not the detail—we still had not committed totally to a direction. Sure, the barnboard idea was okay, and so was the sculpturing of wood, but we still sought a better means of producing and marketing his carvings.

It was on one of our excursions—a simple picnic after fishing—when we discovered the gift. It came in the form of a rotted red pine log that lay sideways on an island. The bark was very much intact. A branch protruding from part of the log had fallen away, leaving an oblong hole where the branch had once been. Jim started pulling away the decayed portions and beckoned me to take a look. It was a beautiful piece, the rich redness of the scaly bark with hues of grey and brown. We began to see where a carving could be placed, in the hole of the bark.

And so, we adopted the "knotty bird." Our eyes were set on wood scoured from around the lake, mostly pine, some diamond willow, some birch with holes—mostly weathered blemishes of nature that would allow Jim to carve a portion of a bird. He could maintain the level of precision and detail that his art demanded by reducing the amount of visible bird. Additional time would need to be spent cleaning and drying the pieces. Additional time would be required in search of the perfect canvas, but it would be a significant reduction to actual carving time.

The lake once more provided, and once more spoke to us. It fed us like we were hungry puppies. We had a huge appetite to grow, and so we were fed. It fed us, as life experiences do when you listen to the messages. She knocked on our door, not with tremendous force, like our first storm, not like the ferocious being of the wild, but with incredible clarity and body. It seemed a gift for our commitment to learn from nature, to endure and persevere. Perhaps we were being tested on how we treated the lake, the islands of Lake of the Woods. She returned a priceless gift. The gift lay before us. Dead and rotting. Pushed and thrown, as random as life itself. It was not worn beaver pulp. It was not the usual driftwood that swept the sandy beaches with its silky, smooth skin. It was deteriorated, it was old, it was weary, it was weathered. It was the root. It was the bark. It was the fallen away. It was the trees on the lake that withered and crashed as storms swept through and spent many years lying still until the forces of nature allowed it to emerge. It held the memories as our parents and grandparents did. A face of leather, deep grooves representing the roadmap of experience, with physical weariness in the depleting life force. Scraggly, twisted tentacles representing the aging arthritic process of limbs, with no more resistance from elements of life. Long after they are gone, the living find the foundation of their own being in the resurfacing of the wood.

CHAPTER 28

THE BEAR

The polished leaves of the poplar, with silvery bark and splotches of black dots, stood stark against the pine backdrop. It was the weekend, and we embarked for our journey around ten a.m. The wind had already kicked up to ten knots, with blotchy blue sky behind heavy clouds. As usual, when planning a day out on the lake, we had to be prepared for any weather. Sekima stood proudly at the bow, tightly curled tail waving feverishly at the smorgasbord of animal smells. As one unusual smell would fade, he would race to the back of the boat as if to savor the odor a little longer.

Jim skirted the shoreline of an island he had been eyeing for some time. It had great possibilities for weather-beaten roots and even interesting driftwood. It ran long and narrow, north to south like most of the big islands did. Their wide faces hung to the east and west, and it was on these westerly shores that most of the floating debris lodged. We had talked about the formation of these islands as the glacier pushed south, scraping and crushing everything in its path. Then it finally receded, gouging deep into the hollows of sediment, leaving the resisting Canadian Shield of rounded granite bases which were the foundation of the islands. There was something safe and secure, knowing and unknown about this four-billion-year-old rock that stood the test of the mighty Ice Age.

Jim parked the boat in a slight gap between two rocks, avoiding the sandy cove. Although the cove promised wooden treasures, we knew many sandy beaches held shallow depths with random boulders lying in wait. Like land mines, they would be just below the surface and could easily damage our prop or even the keel of the boat. I was first out and stepped gingerly onto shore, carefully avoiding the blackened surface of the rock which we knew would be slippery. I grabbed the bow line and tied the boat to a scraggly jack pine. Once told, Sekima was quick to disembark and hightail it into the bush.

There was a random and interesting selection of wood on the shoreline. The perfect specimen to Jim was an unusual piece where he saw an opportunity to place a songbird or raptor. Of particular interest were the roots that had aged like cryptic tombs, thrown and scored by the lake with age and wind. He sought unusual formation and color. The large brush called diamond willow was a treasure. It was strong and grew to a circumference of no more than five or six inches on the banks of the lake. It had two exceptional qualities. Its color was that of a rich, bronzed medallion with hues of grey. But even more distinctive, each branch that broke away from its trunk formed a perfect diamond figure on the surface. Each diamond shape had a series of rings of similar shape and varying depths in the wood. It had surprising qualities for such a commonplace bush.

The silence of our exploration was interrupted by Sekima's titanic bark. He was very worked up about something. On previous adventures, he would investigate the shoreline. It was on the shoreline that he found most small mammals to harass. Jim was down the shoreline from me, as we frequently separated to cover the most distance. Jim pointed above him in the direction of Sekima's growling bark. Whatever the disturbance, we had never heard Sekima so riled. It would be worth hiking the short distance to locate the dog and his new adversary.

I was some distance from Jim and Sekima. I watched Jim disappear into the woods as I hurried my pace to catch up. Sekima's
wail was not letting up, an insistent aggressive tone that led me to
believe it was a larger animal, perhaps even a bear. Jim had told
me that black bears were afraid of dogs, but also that no dog was
a match for the speed and brute force of a bear. One swipe with
those long claws, and a dog would be down or dead.

I was still below Jim by over thirty feet. The islands typically
were fifty to 150 feet high with relatively steep inclines, and often
through dense underbrush including prickly mounds of juniper.
We had made our way through the entanglement of scrub bush
kissing the shoreline and entered a relatively clean area of mixed
birch and pine. Jim had stopped ahead, and I suddenly saw what
he had in his sights. Sekima, still above us on the island slope,
had treed a big black bear. The bear, likely weighing close to four
hundred pounds, had made his way up a large pine tree. Sekima
circled the tree, deep barks and growls keeping the bear wary. The
game for both Sekima and the bear would last until one of them
lost the endurance to continue. Sekima would feign a retreat to
allow the bear to come down a few yards, and then harass it back
up with short, aggressive maneuvers. The big bear was adept at
climbing a tree but not equipped for continuous repetition.

I watched as Jim made his way above the dog and bear for a
better vantage point. Jim whistled. The dog and bear were at a
standoff. I stood frozen, as I was sure that Jim had some kind of
plan to end the standoff. He would intervene before the bear tired
and had to confront Sekima. Sekima was a powerful young, male
malamute with lots of guts, but in Jim's estimation the bear would
win, hands down.

The whistle disrupted Sekima's advances. Acute to sound and
especially the high pierced whistle that signaled him to come, he
retreated, trying to determine what direction to turn. He started

retracing his path downwards towards me. I screamed his name as loudly as I could. The bear was instantly aware that the dog had left. Seizing the moment, it scrambled quickly down the tree. Torn between obeying a command and the drive to confront an opponent, Sekima turned back, his instinct overriding. He had left his prey unattended.

The black bear's choices were limited. Jim had avoided their stance and followed the easiest path up the face of the island so that he had an outlook point in a narrow ravine. With Sekima in hot pursuit, the bear now tracked the same path towards Jim, following the contour of the ravine. The speed of a black bear can be upwards of sixty miles per hour for short distances. The bear, with its massive head dipping with each lunge forward, hurtled itself up the hill, crashing through sapling and underbrush as though it was whipped cream. He was headed for a collision course with Jim.

I could see all of it happening, helpless to do anything but watch. Jim had nowhere to go. I could see him snugged up against a large boulder in the small channel. He certainly could not outrun the bear. The bear would be upon him in seconds with Sekima right behind. Without a doubt, Sekima was an alpha male. He was fearless and intelligent. He had already responded to us as though we were a Pack. Jim's presence would only accelerate an attack should the bear slow.

I saw Jim pick up a heavy branch without hesitating. As the bear reached him on the one-way path, he swung, clipping the bear in the face, forcing him to climb sideways, toppling young saplings, stripping moss and undergrowth from granite. Had the bear not been retreating from Sekima, he may have confronted Jim. The bear chose to move faster, its black glimmering coat, its layered fat rocking back and forth, swinging back towards the path that led upwards.

It paid no attention to Jim or the log that slapped it. It wanted nothing to do with Jim or the dog that pursued it. It would likely be to the end of this fifty-acre island and swimming across to the next in less than five minutes.

I saw Sekima hesitate as he realized Jim was there, just long enough for Jim to grab the scruff of his neck and chain, halting the dog abruptly. Jim kept a tight hold on him as he half-dragged, half-scrambled down the island slope to where I stood. I had not realized that I was shivering, not from the fresh morning air, but the fear that one or both of my guys was going to be hurt.

Jim kept a tight hold on the dog until we were back in the boat. He was not about to follow Sekima the length of the island in pursuit of a long-gone black butt.

Sekima was anxious and pacing. Jim was making nothing of the whole thing. And I was reliving every moment. I could practically feel the hot breath of the bear on my neck. I imagined how it smelled, like rotting dirt and rancid meat. I was ready to go home. Most of the time, our excursions were blessed with a few beautiful pieces of a wood for Jim's carvings. Sometimes, though, that just was not possible on the lake.

CHAPTER 29

MIXED CULTURE

It became obvious that we had multiple dynamics of cultural differences that we connected with and that we were experiencing. It was a strange sensation, but not particularly unusual for either of us. There was a group of vacation people that owned islands, and they were primarily Americans. There were local business people that lived meager during winter months and charged accordingly for the short months of summer, determined to live in this wild paradise. They were a mix of US landed immigrants and Canadians. There was a significant Indigenous (Ojibway) population that had been separated by reservation and culture. We interacted in different ways. Many guided for the resort where I worked. I knew them by name, and we mingled on a regular basis. Jim occasionally guided at the resort as a private contractor, so had varying relationships. There was an additional group, a transient working group of individuals from all walks of life, that came to the resort for summer employment. It was a diverse group of people, as diverse and unique as the lake itself.

The serenity of island living and Jim's solid character provided the stability that I needed in a chaotic and confusing work environment. Highly intelligent, a Mensa member and an educated son of affluent parents, Jim had an uncanny ability to judge intent. Content meant very little to Jim. Intent was far more important. It was not surprising that as I brought each saga of my work surroundings home, Jim recognized the pattern of the owners' manipulation and steered me clear.

Fortunately, I had very little confrontation with Donald for a long time. I waited. I presented timely financial reports, and Donald did not want anything to do with boring number crunching. The summer was a crazy busy time, but I had streamlined the department so that I could efficiently do what was required, and more, in a five-day work week. Carlie was unhappy that I had attained the right. Donald did not care because it was being done more efficiently and accurately than ever before.

Donald was interested in hands-on management of people, from servers to housekeepers to store retail clerks and guests. He trusted no one, except for a handful—his loyal, faithful servants and his children. His children were elevated to positions beyond their experience and bore the same arrogance and egotism. They were helpless to know the difference and did not want to. I kept my head down, professional, disinterested in the drama, and he left me alone.

Seasonally hired managers of the various departments quickly learned that they had no authority over their staff. Donald would continuously change the rules for his personal appetite. If they attempted to employ their own management style that was problematic to his desires, they were dismissed. They left on the same Greyhound bus that they had arrived on. He would have them replaced with someone from that same department, possibly with no skills at all. Firing was a common occurrence. The new manager would have learned to tell Donald how wonderful he was, how smart and funny. After all, he was the supreme authority.

The largest turnover was always in the dining room. The majority of servers were scheduled for evening, as breakfast was a buffet, and lunch was a traditional shore lunch—a fish fry on the lake facilitated by fishing guides or dock crew.

Donald would leave prior to lunch, in his boat equipped with coolers of pop, beer, champagne, hors d'oeuvres trays, and extra fishing bait. A handful of servers who were pleasing to the eye went along for the ride. Giggling and laughing in bikini tops and short jean shorts, they would make their way down the dock to Donald's deep hull Lund, ecstatic that they were going for a boat ride on the lake. They would flash smiles and flesh while serving the resort guests at various shore lunch spots dotted about on the lake on public lands. The whole round trip was no more than three hours, which would put them back at the resort around two p.m. Most of the time, it would be three or four p.m. Long enough to get the girls drunk. Their squeals of laughter were audible. Donald would head to his island home for a break, his big Lund leaving a wake that would hit the docks and send the girls falling into each other as they tried to keep their balance. Those scheduled for dining room service would miss their five o'clock shift, sending the dining room manager into a frenzy. Attempts to discipline the girls for missing a shift were placated by Donald. He would simply imply that it was better to let the girls have a little fun than be so tough on them. They were doing a great job. For him.

By mid-summer, there was only one thing left on everyone's mind: finish the season. Employees had been promised a bonus that was part of a shared tip fund. If they quit or got fired, it was lost. By now, they had little to show for their efforts. Thirty percent of their minimum wage was eaten up by their room and board. I was finally able to get an agreement from Donald that we set a maximum purchase amount on employees' tabs. The payroll software could not digest a negative check, and I found myself having to rework the staff charges to come up with a zero balance after taxes. They were trapped in a party culture that Donald fostered for his own profit and entertainment. They could drink at the bar. They could buy expensive sporty fishing clothes in the store. They could buy cigarettes, pop, chips, novelty items. All of the items were overpriced. They were all priced in American dollars, inflated for the tourists that would be vacationing there. If they made it to the end of the season, all they would likely take home was the bonus they had been promised. The bonus that could be arbitrarily changed at Donald's discretion. The power and control he had over staff were deliberate, measured, and overwhelmingly intended to pad his pockets. He made himself believe that he was the creator of the best party these people would ever have in their lifetime. At their expense.

I waited. I waited when he was seething with rage. I waited when he blamed others for a mistake not of their doing. I waited when he glorified himself. I stayed silent. I stayed focus on doing my job in my little accounting world. I was one person in a culture filled with vanity. An evil man who exploited the young, the innocent, the uneducated, the misguided, and the misfits, by encouraging them to be a family of sorts, with common goals and common themes. They were finally belonging to something, adapting to fit in. He encouraged them to abandon their sexual morality, their work ethics, their responsibility to finances. He encouraged them to deceive themselves. They were to be loyal and protect him at all costs. What was at great risk was their fragile self-worth. If they did not fit in to the culture, they could be humiliated and abandoned once again.

I knew he was evil; he was darkness. I waited.

CHAPTER 30

FISHIN' AND SWIMMIN'

The challenges of a crazy nepotistic family fishing resort could not dampen my summer spirits. The progress we made on our island home, a little bit at a time, was significant to me. We had no employment when we arrived. Now we had my regular monthly income, and Jim had combined his carving skills with his guiding skills on the lake to make our monthly payments doable. We had bare minimum, but we had everything. We had a roof over our heads and food on our table, including plenty of fish. We had the lake. We were already working on a plan for an addition, incorporating a real bathroom, utility, and master bedroom. We were hoping that Paul could do the foundation work that required equipment, and we would do much of the framing and finishing. We looked at late fall for a start. It might take a few years to complete, but we thought we could get started.

Our little abode was not what made our paradise. It was the lake. Lake of the Woods is one of the world's best fishing grounds. Sixteen thousand islands, 64,000 miles of shoreline, and a basin that looks like the Appalachians, through the Midwest plateaus and valleys to the Rocky Mountains. Pinnacles and bowls. The Lake of the Woods was designed well by the Ice Age, all the islands running southeast and northwest as the glaciers sculptured.

The lake's diversity required years of experience for comfortable navigation and so many more years to understand its structure below that blue beauty. We were experiencing a love affair that would last for our lifetime.

We dove off the dock deck. Finally, the lake temperatures had reached about 70°F. On our part of the lake, that could change at a moment's notice. Did I say lake temperatures of 70°F at the upper two feet? Below that, depending on which way the wind was blowing, the temperature could be 50° to 60°. Our swimming platform went into sixty-foot depths, while the south side of the island was over two hundred feet deep.

Sekima dove in after us. A healthy, big malamute with webbed feet from a labrador mother or father. It was easy to be lured back to the water when summer temperatures finally reached above 80°F. For most Canadians, that's hot. We were already aware that Sekima would swim over three hundred yards to Channel Island, north of us, just for the fun of it. We usually caught him before he made the commitment. Beyond twenty feet, and no amount of yelling, calling, or screaming would turn his head. It was then that we would be concerned that he would be struck by an oncoming boat. We were already resting on the deck from our early evening swim when we saw it. So did Sekima.

A black bear emerged from the underbrush on Channel Island. Sekima plunged into the water ignoring our commands, his broad head just above the surface, effortlessly paddling with long smooth thrusts. The bear appeared to be a two-year old, the size of a fifty-five-gallon drum. It saw Sekima coming and it paused to look sideways as it made its way down the shoreline. It was a rare sight as black bear with their incredible sense of smell have no reason to ever be seen. It can smell decaying carcass up to twenty miles away. It reminded me of how this incredible animal of nature was hunted primarily for trophy, baited with rancid grease and rotten meat. Its existence for food had been discarded many years ago.

Sekima made it across the bay safely. We watched as the bear continued to waddle down the shoreline, fat from summer foraging. Sekima kept pace with it, swimming about five feet from the rocky shore. He was clearly at a disadvantage, nervous about being attacked by the bear when exiting the water. Occasionally the bear would stop, slap the water with a clawed paw. The bear had traveled the width of Channel and appeared tired of the game. Without looking back, it made its way into the bush and was gone. Sekima chose not to follow instead changing course and headed back home.

Summer was alive with activity. The tiniest of warbler nests hidden in the bushes emptied of fledglings. From the deck we had watched a doe and her two fawns come to the water's edge on Channel Island. As we watched through binoculars, she lifted her nose to the air, big ears working independently gaging any hidden threat. Eagles spiraled to the ground, talons locked, tumbling to possible death. A lone bull moose suddenly aware of our presence lifted its elongated head, water plants spilling from its bulbous muzzle, nostrils flaring. The wonders of nature, its incredible wisdom and beauty, its timelessness, its complexity, its simplicity. We were such a small part of its magnificence.

CHAPTER 31

CAP MAN

We sat on our front deck, a beautiful fall night with that brilliant combination of deep orange and purple. It was cold enough to wear a jacket, and perhaps later we would entertain a small fire to take the chill from the air. It was not the pastel colors of a spring night. It was the depth of the autumnal equinox, with blackened edges as the sun retreated. It was a night that promised brilliant stars and moon. If you were on the lake, you had best know the constellation you were heading towards. The lake and trees would become merely slippery shadows.

I was not sure how to lead up to the conversation with Jim. Donald had announced that he was taking all the Managers on a three-night stay to Minnesota, after the resort closed in September. He was renting a luxury bus, and all expenses would be paid. I was torn. It had been some time since I had gone anywhere. Some of the people that were going I genuinely liked. If I did not go, I would be one of the chosen few to keep the office running, while everyone else had four days off.

I explained the offer to Jim and got the answer I expected.

"So, it's a big party, with lots of drinking and smoking. You know that would be a big temptation for you."

He was right. Almost everyone at the resort smoked, and occasionally I would break down and have a cigarette. "It doesn't seem fair," I said. "I'd have to work while everyone else has fun."

"Tell him you have other plans then, and you can't work either." Jim had that stern look on this face that told me I was not making a convincing case. I knew I was not. "Who all is going?"

I named a few, and Jim shook his head. "I thought you said this was for Managers only. Why would Tom and Steve be invited?"

I knew the answer, and it made things even worse. They were party animals. Donald loved to have them around for the entertainment.

"You do whatever you want. It's up to you."

I knew the decision I needed to make. Many people were trying to get me to go, but it wasn't a good idea for me. Would I drink? Yes. Would I end up smoking? Probably.

We sat in silence in our own thoughts. It was serene and tranquil. It made putting things into perspective a lot easier. Something caught Jim's eye.

"What do you think that guy is doing?" He did not have to tell me where. He was looking straight to the west at a small island.

Not a quarter mile beyond, we saw him walking back and forth, occasionally touching the bill of his cap with contemplation. Had he not been pacing we likely would not have noticed at all. The island was a mere speck, less than a good size city lot.

"Oh crap. He's gathering wood like he's going to make a fire. If you look through the trees there, he's got a little open boat." I could not imagine why he would be trying to build a fire, other than he intended on spending the night. We had not heard his boat, which meant that he had been there for a while, since before we came out on the deck a half hour before.

"So why do you think that he pulled up to that little island when he can practically touch the other island that is over fifty acres? He might have a bit more firewood for the night."

"We can't just leave him there."

"Oh, really. It's an interesting watch, though, isn't it?" Jim practically chuckled. He was not in the mood for a rescue.

"It's not that funny."

"Tell me, why not? Here's a guy with a broken-down boat, way too small for this part of the lake, wearing a ball cap and sweat pants, at dusk, in the fall, collecting sticks for a fire that should last about fifteen minutes."

"You're right. It is funny because we can sit and watch from over here. What do you think he's going to do next?" I played along. It was the first time I had observed a real survival moment that was not my own. It wasn't like those TV survival shows that make it appear as though there is a survival crisis when really someone is always there to save them. Nature just does not work that way. There is no one in the background ready to save you. When faced with survival in nature, humans need to work together to overcome. Sometimes, there is no way out, but a Pack has a better chance of survival. This is the reason wolves, elephants, and geese stay with their Pack. But separated from the Pack, all alone, your likelihood of survival is significantly diminished.

We had gotten our binoculars out, and could see that the interior of the open sixteen-foot boat had a fishing rod, a gas can, and a life jacket. No blanket, no jacket, no backpack, an empty void. Here he is, totally out of his element, with only his ball cap and sweat pants. It was plain stupid. And so, yes, there was a part of me that did not mind watching things unfold for someone who had total disregard for their own well-being and the seriousness of being ill-equipped on the lake in the fall. Stupid at the highest level.

The sun disappears quickly in the fall, and not long after, dusk whispered. I did not have the heart anymore.

"It's close to dusk. We have to help him."

"Crap. Idiot. He's not staying here tonight. I'm getting that boat going so he can go home, wherever that is."

"You want me to come with you?"

"No point. I'm taking a tank of gas with me. I hope that's all it is. That better fix it."

Jim was there within a few minutes. I drank my wine. It was still a beautiful night. I saw the little boat roar from the island and Jim speeding back to the boathouse. I watched as the Cap Man sped away. By the time Jim reached the deck and explained that he had run out of gas, we saw Cap Man's boat come back into our vision. It had roared off, and we'd both thought that was the end of it, but now it reappeared like a bad rash. It was drifting in the wind and was coming right back at us. We watched him struggle with the tiller, pulling frantically at the starter cord.

I had flashbacks of our own ignorance that first fall, with me getting lost on the island, and a similar reluctant motor. But then I remembered the amount of safeguard we had, the food, the blankets, the extra gasoline. This was not the same at all. But it reminded me how vulnerable and how ridiculous you feel when Mother Nature strips you of the basics. The tiller started and the little boat sped away once more.

It was the end of our discussion. My mind was made up. I would not be going. I would be no more equipped than Cap Man, but I could not plead ignorance. I knew the potential consequences for me personally. I knew that I would be supporting Donald's indulgence. I had almost fallen into a trap.

CHAPTER 32

THE BOG

It was that time of the year again, squirrels busy burying pine cones in the ground, beavers stealing poplar saplings from our shoreline, the water on the lake growing dense and greyish in color. The smell in the air had changed. There was that familiar odor of death and decay, as leaves of shrubs lay stacked uniformly across the earth to decompose. We were more prepared than the first winter. Or so it seemed.

We had cut and piled birch that would last us through to the end of January. We hired Paul to build us an ice road, as I would be driving to and from work during the winter. Jim had ordered a semi-tractor load of birch that was being delivered to a yard in town. He would work from there, cut, split, and haul the wood on the ice road with our little Dodge Dakota. We had traded our boat again, this time for a used Sylvan with a full top and inboard motor. I would push the limit crossing the lake until I could no longer. It all depended on how quickly the bay where I docked froze over. The big waters around us on the island would stay open far beyond the shallow bay. I had arranged to take time off during freeze-up, sometime over December, into the first or second week of January. By then, there would be enough ice for me to ski to town. Part of my employment contract was to have a place to stay at one of the resort's cabins during freeze-up and breakup, but we were doing everything we could to stay on the island.

It was hunting season for white-tailed deer and moose. We had found some trails on the neighboring two-hundred-acre island that lay across from us. It was far too large for us to do any chasing. Before daybreak, we parked our boat and scurried upwards to the top of the island, some two hundred yards to the top, flashlights strobing our footing as we went. We hoped that deer would follow their traditional pattern of meandering and browsing along the trails they had established.

We found two locations, approximately a quarter mile from each other, where we would sit—this is known as still hunting. My spot was behind a large toppled pine tree, its root exposed, having ripped the ball of earth and rocks with it. I could sit on the large trunk and peer through to the deer trail through a portion of the root that was free from debris.

A week earlier, we had come with Sekima attempting to find possible deer activity on the big island. By accident, we followed a ravine to its basin that sliced the island in two. The upward climb on the other side was steeper and treacherous, with jagged cuts of granite. The rock was thick with moss from its growth beneath the filtered light of soaring pine that grew precariously on the edge of the shelf above. Beyond that ravine, we noticed a hollow in the trees, a void before the familiar skyline of heavily-laden black spruce, their tops impregnated with growth and cones. It signaled a change in vegetation that was worth exploring, as we were on the very top of the island and yet this void was leading us downward, away from the shoreline.

Unlike the ravine, descending the slope was relatively gentle and smooth. The pines had grown thicker, and although they were as tall as the spruce on the horizon, the elevation downward made it only seem that they did not exist from afar. The floor became softer, with thick moss that sprang back to its original form with each step. We recognized that we were about to make a discovery. The air became stagnant, a faint smell of musty growth. Suddenly the moss gave way, and we found ourselves grappling to hang onto the nearest tree as our running shoes became submerged in brackish water. The ground had leveled off, and it appeared we were coming to the end of one world and the beginning of another. We carefully stepped from spruce to spruce, hanging on the edges of stable roots.

We emerged to a wide opening of low mossy covering, void of trees, with a sphagnum bog at its center. We stepped gingerly onto this new surface, one hand still securely grasping a tree. Rather than break through to water, it held our weight, although it moved as though it was firm gelatin. It trembled and wobbled beneath our steps. We tried quick knee bends and watched the mossy surface ripple. We were walking on thick vegetation that floated on the brackish water.

Quick to take advantage of a swim, Sekima jumped into the pool. We realized that there was no shoreline of rock or sand that sloped. He was immediately swimming. There was no telling how deep it was. Its color was dark tamarack brown, the same color as the peat moss that made up the basin. It was like looking into a black hole. The delicate fabric below our feet was made up of small tentacles and, on closer observation, we recognized the dainty plant and fruit of wild cranberry. We walked the edge of a portion of the bog, now able to see a defined ridge that would offer a more stable walkway back. We found the elusive and rare pitcher plant that was certain to be the explosive surprise evil in a horror movie about a man-eating plant. It looked like an open-toed slipper, attracting and funneling its prey into a rich, sticky liquid. Long spines grew downward to prevent the fly from being able to escape. The carnivorous plant digests its protein meal in its liquid stomach.

Although we had come to the island to assess deer movement

and population, we had discovered a treasure and wonder of the world. Over the years, we returned to this miraculous creation of nature, ever careful to not disturb the fragile ecosystem. Its delicate formation would not have been sustainable to human traffic, and so it was, in nature's intelligence, hidden from view.

Returning to hunt, the first signs of light I saw were from the east filtering through the trees, although not yet enough for me to see any distance along the deer path. I had not moved an inch since I sat on the trunk, except for my toes within my boots, my fingers, and my head. It was barely above freezing temperatures, and the heat of the walk in had dissipated. I knew from experience that even the smallest of movement would be captured by a wary white-tail. I moved my head ever so slightly, counting seconds between the slightest movement, working my eyes to catch as much peripheral vision as possible.

There was no sound this morning. The spruce and jack pine forest were not home to birds or small rodents. The familial chattering of a squirrel or jay was nonexistent. It was replaced with a tranquility and silence typical to the depths of earth or space. I waited, but not long.

At first it was merely a break in the silence, a sound too far away to recognize direction or pattern. I focused on the sound. It seemed to fade in and out, or was it stopping and starting? I could hear it more rhythmically now. The sound was intensifying, coming my way. The earth here was rock, much of it covered with short bushes, juniper, blueberries, scrub jack pine and red pine. It was not like hunting amidst oak with drying leaves that crackled underfoot. The sound was louder, closer, but interrupted for long periods as the earth cover was a soundless barrier.

Finally, after what seemed an eternity, I could hear the animal from somewhere behind me. I had experienced deer coming from opposite directions before. But this sounded rushed, in a hurry, chasing, or being chased. Even the bounding of a deer would be quieter than what I was hearing. I had seen large and small animals in the bush and was not concerned that I was in danger. Whatever it was, it was not coming for me. I was not being stalked.

It was on me now. Some twenty feet off my left shoulder, I could hear it running. There he was. Sekima, water-streaked wolf coat, running at a strong lope, a glance my way and veering towards where Jim would be sitting. He had swum the three hundred yards from our island, following our scent, and was ensuring that he located both other Pack members. The Pack had now finished the unsuccessful hunt.

CHAPTER 33

COMPASS

By now I have had numerous lessons on the use of a compass. I had worked in a surveyor's office when I was younger, and of course I likely knew a bit more about direction than many. That did not mean I knew anything about using a compass, like my Eagle Scout partner. Over time, the compass gave me the confidence I needed to navigate the zig-zagged islands that we hunted. It was apparent with the settling in of fall that I would need the compass to navigate the waters as well.

Dense fog blanketed the lake some mornings, reducing visibility to less than two hundred feet. Because of the blending effect of fog and shadows to the naked eye, it would appear that visibility was much less, somewhere at twenty feet. Of course, there were always varying degrees of density. We chose one morning where we could see a vague outline of the neighboring island for a lesson on driving the boat in fog.

We had installed a marine compass in the boat. A marine compass is quite different than a land compass. It reminds me of a snow globe, the little scene encapsulated in fluid. You shake it, and the little sparkles inside are carried by the water and float down like snowflakes. The marine compass is a globe filled with liquid, allowing for the adjustment required as a result of the up and down movement of the boat.

The first five hundred yards was relatively easy. I could make out the shoreline of the big island to my left. I was up on step and the boat had planed out at a relatively low speed of twenty miles per hour.

"So, you know your heading is fifty degrees northeast," Jim reminded me. "Just maintain that heading and you will see Honeymoon Island in a few minutes."

"I've got it. Exactly fifty degrees Northeast." My hand tightly gripped the throttle. We had left the comforting shores of the big island, and we were in the open big waters of Whitefish Bay. There was no land to be seen in any direction. I suddenly felt panic, with one of my senses being totally removed. My eyesight had no meaning, no bearing, a total void of image, a greyish white cloud encapsulating all of me, like being trapped inside a darkened room with no windows. Only I was moving at considerable speed. Suddenly I panicked and pulled back on the throttle. The bow lifted and we were no longer on step. My mind was abuzz.

"What are you doing?"

"I can't do this."

"You can't go at this speed. You'll lose your bearing. You're not going fast enough."

The marine compass needle drifted erratically this way and that, more than ten degrees, one way, then the other, as I tried to compensate. I looked about at the dense fog and felt adrift, fluid, and out of control.

"I can't do it." I shook my head in fear and defeat.

"Okay. Get out of the seat before we've lost all our bearings." Jim said, frustration creeping into his voice. "You know you have to get over this. You won't just run into an island, even in this fog."

"It doesn't feel that way." I shifted over to the passenger side of the boat as he grabbed the steering wheel.

"I've told you before. You have to trust the compass. It's your heading."

The boat was on step now, Jim pursuing the fifty-degree north-east course. A few minutes later we saw an island to our bow. It was Honeymoon. Although it lay to the port side, not the starboard, as we had anticipated, it could be nothing else. The same symmetrical pattern, and the only island that we would see before mainland.

"See, now how hard is that." It was more a statement than a question. "You know where you are, don't you?"

"Yes, of course. I got *really* scared."

And so, I did not hesitate the next time, or the next time. To help me out, we timed how long it would take at twenty miles per hour to reach Honeymoon. I had three exact changes of direction. After I left the boathouse to the corner of the big island Channel, to Honeymoon, and an alternate direction for the final approach to the bridge in town. I would go much slower on that final approach as there were buoy markers, but in heavy fog even they were difficult to locate.

I would not say it was like riding a bicycle, or even maneuvering through a maze. It was more like a pilot flying with only instruments, awaiting the lights on the runway. I was no pilot, however, and each morning that arrived with fog, I felt nausea and unease in my stomach until I parked on mainland. The fog would dissipate before noon, and the return trip was never blind. I had overcome my paralysis.

One morning, I could barely make out the big island. I knew the depths of its shoreline were safe for me to follow, and I did that morning, at a slow pace.

The fog rose like steam out of the lake. It moved and shifted, drawing abstract ghost-like figures. It is no wonder that Windigo folklore was created by Algonquin-speaking First Nations in North America. Paddling long stretches of water with shape-shifting creatures, one would naturally fear for their life. Some got lost and did not survive the elements. They did not return to their homes, and so it was that Windigo was created. Believed to have been a lost hunter, Windigo was forced to become a cannibalistic spirit creature. It was as rare as Bigfoot; fog over the lake was a perfect cover for this unsightly beast.

When I reached the gap that indicated I would need to be on my fifty-degree heading, I pushed the throttle forward. On step, I pulled back so that I clocked twenty miles per hour. I was tense. It would be exactly four minutes before I would see Honeymoon. The fog was so heavy it covered my windshield as though I was in a downpour. The inside was no better, with a heavy film of dew. Resisting the temptation to slow the boat down, I maintained my speed with one hand on the wheel, attempting to open the canvas top with the other. The boat was fully enclosed and I wanted to be able to see Honeymoon. I needed to stand up with my head above the windshield and the canopy. It was often necessary in evening travel for better visibility. It was now crucial in these conditions. My heart raced as I stole glances below to verify my heading. My hair was wet. I felt a cold chill as it soaked through.

It seemed too long to me. I had a general time frame, not like a stopwatch. I was definitely within the range of four to six minutes, so where was Honeymoon? Land. I saw an island, and then another. I pulled back on the throttle. Had I made it past Honeymoon without noticing? Was this the entrance into the bay before the bridge? There were several islands in there, but I hadn't really paid that much attention to their shape or configuration as I relied on the buoys.

No. There were more islands, dotting the landscape both port and starboard. There were far too many, and they were too small. I had gone off course. I felt nauseous again. Panic, fear. I dared not move the boat in anticipation that I would come in contact with one of the many reefs that lay just below the water. Even at idle, the boat would not stay in one position. I put it in gear, and started doing tight circles to give myself time to regroup.

It felt too similar to that time when I was lost on the island we'd hunted. Waves of doubt. Streams of internal chatter. I couldn't believe I was here again. At least I had some recollection of what lay north and south. North were large islands with a narrow gap that would have been impossible for me to passage through without seeing shoreline on either side. If I was south, there were many small islands, but how far south was I? I tried studying the navigational map, but although the fog was lifting, the formation of the islands was distorted. I had no way of retracing my path as I had obviously veered off the fifty-degree northeast while opening the boat canvas. At what degree, and for how long, was just a guess.

I had plenty of gas. I was not going to risk an unknown course. I continued to do circles, judging my position by the distance from the islands, from right to left. There was nothing to do but wait for the fog to lift. Why was so much of life about waiting? Why so much of life without knowing exactly the direction to be taken? It seemed the smallest of deviation could lead to unchartered territory in life. Once, I had been mad and spontaneously quit a job, without another option which led to months of waiting for responses from an untold number of interviews. There were many other moments like this. Deviation of my life path in such a short time.

What prices were paid when I did not wait, but reacted impulsively because I wanted things to go faster? Wait in line. Wait on hold. Wait for the oven to warm up. Wait for the date that is always late. When is a good time to wait? A good time to wait was now.

I wanted so badly to move, to do something, but I knew better. Unlike when I was lost before, there was no rescue. I was on my own. Unlike before, I was surer of myself. It didn't mean that I was not terrified. I kept those doubtful voices at bay. I let the swirls of doubt dissipate in the fog. I let my experience dictate. I trusted nature to lift the veil. I also knew that there were still many unchartered courses when I would have to make a decision – to wait or push ahead.

The sun was burning off the fog. I would likely be late for work, but it was a small price to pay when the alternative was potentially losing the lower end of my motor on a rock. I curved around again, always clockwise, always checking that distance from the nearest shore. I saw it then. Tucked in a small cove on one of the islands was a dock with a boat tied up. It was just what I needed. There could be someone at their summer cabin. Someone that could tell me where I was and even how to get to the bridge and town. There was enough visibility now that if I stood in the boat, above its canvas and windshield, I could see below the surface of the water. It would not suffice at any great speed, but I could slowly make my way over to the dock. There was no guarantee that there were not reefs in front of their island, so I set forth at snail's pace.

Within twenty-five feet of the dock, I saw a woman descending the stairs, clad in a brilliantly-colored kimono-style dress. I was convinced this was my one and only opportunity and frantically waved, honked, and belted out hello's. She really didn't have any choice but to notice me.

"I got lost in the fog and do not know where I am," I yelled loudly. "Can you hear me?"

"Yes. There is a reef off to your right side. Come in this way." She drew a circle that was not definitive to me. I was not about to mess things up now. "You are close to town." she yelled.

"Am I south of town? How do you get to town from here?"

She pointed. "Through the gap there, or go around all of these islands and you will see the mainland. Follow the mainland to Sanctuary Lodge. You know the way from there?"

I was positively ecstatic. I would not go through the gap. Leave that to the island people that use the back way. I was going back into the waters that I knew. I was not that far off track. Just enough to have created a lot of trouble. Here we go again. Just like life, sometimes the dial setting is just a little off, a bit of fine tuning, a small measured turn of the knob, and you're back on course.

Morning coffee in her hand, black hair threading down to her shoulders, intense pink, yellow, and aqua-colored dress to her calves, she was a sunrise sun goddess to me. I waved over my shoulder as the boat lunged onto step. Afraid or not, I would make it through the murky vapor.

CHAPTER 34

LOYAL SUBJECTS

It was Friday, the last day of our relief from Donald. He was away and would return Monday morning. Getting lost in the fog had cost me an extra half hour, and my adrenalin was still pumping.

The season had ended at the Resort. There was an emptiness to the place. Seasonal staff that had forged a new family hugged and cried, sharing phone numbers and addresses, and finally scattering, some with their own cars, most with bus tickets. The party bus to Minneapolis had returned with stories not to be shared. What happens on the party bus, stays on the party bus. Now, a few staff remained at the resort, including myself. There would be various construction workers over the winter, payrolls, and leases, insurance reviews, and banking to keep me busy. A skeleton staff of three or four was kept to do reservations. Carlie would start the process of inventory and re-ordering and oversee reservations.

The fishing guides were gone. The boats and motors were being returned to a marina to be assessed for damages. Donald had already started the long drawn-out fight over costs incurred from damages and leases to be signed. Although he had no program for reducing damages caused by neglect or inexperienced guides, he fervently argued that the marina was ripping him off when it came time to fix them. Predictably, he was not proactive but reactive to circumstances. Although he could not identify exactly how he was being ripped off, he insisted that they were out to get him.

There was little that I could do but try to negotiate lower rates for the size of the account, or fixed rates for certain recurring items. To ensure that there was not some devious plotting, I recommended a damage sheet on each boat be prepared, with pictures, if necessary, before they were returned, and coordinate with the marina to sign off. It had limited success. There were so few people available at the end of the season and returning the boats became a flurry of disorganized activity.

The culture of the resort had been formed many years prior to my employment. At the top of the chain was Donald. His children sought and received the financial gain, authority without ever having gained experience, and indeed were the most loyal to him. Then Carlie. Then other loyal subjects. Those subjects consisted of a handful of men that would do whatever was asked of them, regardless of how degrading or unreasonable. They had little or no education. Some lacked basic hygiene. They drank and smoked, lived pay check to pay check, and had nowhere and no one to go to other than their Nutt family. The Nutt family could make embarrassing jokes about them in front of part-time summer staff, scream or yell at them, call them "stupid" or "idiot," but still call upon them day or night for an errand. They lived in shacks at the resort and were on call 24/7. They were incredibly inept at the positions they were given, always with a title but with insignificant pay—but they were loyal. For that loyalty, they were allowed to be included in the family Christmas or birthday celebrations. For their devotion, they occasionally experienced offerings of kindness—not unlike a master bestowing kindness upon a slave. They were expected to be grateful.

By the very nature of authoritative power and control, Donald was always having to test and sometimes reestablish loyalty. Something was bigger than him. There was some other influence that threatened to destabilize his authority. I could see it in small ways. His subjects had something beyond what he could ever control. There was an internal defense against what he represented. It came through their connections to others.

The operation required over a hundred employees from various backgrounds and influences, thrown into the mix. They communicated, linked together over three meals a day and close quarters, with comradery, with hope, with strengths and weaknesses. From the chef that slipped food into empty backpacks to late night boat joy rides, and flagrant parties by his own children that dipped into his profits, there was rebellion.

Many Indigenous guides were distrustful, people he could not control. Some stole from him and pretended they were loyal. They laughed at him as they indulged in their good fortune of stolen coolers, boat paddles, life jackets, pop, and food.

Donald was only one man who attempted to manipulate and control. There was a greater force that was inconceivable and unrecognizable – another influence was always at play. As the season ended, so did some of that energy as it dissipated like fading light. Donald could now concentrate his efforts on fewer people.

There were a series of trade shows throughout the United States that were a major marketing tool for sporting goods and vacation destinations. Sports shows that captured the attention of potential fishing guests had already begun. Donald was at one of those now and we all enjoyed the reprieve from the constant chaos that he created.

During the summer, Donald preferred the excitement he created amidst young staffers and the lavish praise of guests. He avoided the dry administration of an office setting. Many guests had won a corporate contest for a three day get away, likely only ever dreaming of such a prize as the Canadian North, fishing on Lake of the Woods. Donald would be seen on the dock each morning at six a.m. to capture their excitement as the fleet headed out to the fishing grounds. This was his empire, and he took great pleasure in letting guests know he was the exclusive mastermind of all of it.

With the resort closed, he was at the helm in the office. There was no way of getting away from the daily uproar he relished in creating. The sports shows could be three days or all week affairs. Things went so smoothly when he was not around.

That morning, Carlie greeted me. Without his influence, she was a different person. She could be funny and spontaneous and let her guard down. She quickly let me know what her morning discussion with Donald had been like. She had started to see that I was not a threat to her position, and perhaps in some small ways I had demonstrated compassion for her plight. Although not physically present, he would predictably call two minutes after the office opened, and two minutes before it closed. He was upset this morning. That usually meant he wasn't getting the results he expected. Perhaps a corporate CEO deciding to take his group golfing instead of fishing. Perhaps someone said something that sounded critical of him. Anything slightly unfavorable he took as an extreme, personal hostile attack.

It seems that morning, he was faced with a call from a corporate CEO that wanted specific guides, specific dates, and specific accommodations. Donald had spoken to one of the reservation girls, Beverly, about it, and had her working on it. He had called at seven a.m., an hour before the office opened. She had become like one of the other subjects. If Beverly was to work at the resort, she and her young child needed accommodations. It meant Donald would have a reservation clerk 24/7. It meant that he had found another loyal subject based on their survival needs.

She had a chart of what had already been reserved, as many of the corporate clients made those bookings when they were leaving.

Beverly was instructed by Donald to talk to the CEO and provide him with the itinerary to meet his specifics. She did come up with a certain number of requirements, but not all. Several of the top guides were already booked, and some of the requested cabins were already booked. Carlie explained to me that Beverly was already in a closed-door phone call with Donald, and he sounded very angry.

Beverly was a pretty woman, long, straight, dark hair, large brown eyes, and a slender, freckled face. Everything about her was slender. There were times when I could think she was anorexic but she didn't relish being slim. She was always nervous and on edge. Perhaps it was because she was a single mom with a five-year old, with no support from anyone. Again, Donald had found someone that had nowhere to go, who had no one. Sometimes she could be annoying because she talked so much, as though she was trying to build some kind of comfort for herself, but really, she was just a mom who lived in fear.

The door to Donald's office opened. The office where she'd been told to take the call. She stood there, tears running down her face. Sobs vibrated her body. "He fired me." She was crying uncontrollably. She stood wringing her hands and shaking violently. "I have to be out this weekend."

There we were, the five of us. Beverly, two other reservations clerks, Carlie, and myself. We stood paralyzed. We had heard the details of what had happened through Carlie. We all knew that Beverly had provided the best possible guides and accommodations to meet the dates that the CEO required. It was not perfect, but it was always difficult to accommodate every detail that a large group requested. She had been instructed to talk directly with the CEO. As I saw it, she should have phoned Donald first to ask him how he wanted to proceed, given that the request could be only partially met. She was not that savvy. I did not see anyone other than myself or Carlie who knew Donald's volatile personality to understand that this was a no-win situation. It had to be laid out on Donald's terms. It would have to have been him that made the decision to prioritize one guest over another. Here was a company, one boss, one owner who had no training manual for reservations, no policies, who had hired someone he could use over someone who was skilled. Worse yet, the direction for prioritization of clientele was erratic. It was based on Donald's feelings towards the CEO, how he became crazed by any criticism, or how he was swayed by compliments.

I was the first to act. There was only one thing to do. Beverly was clearly on the edge of an emotional breakdown. She lived in a small apartment that was connected to the office. It was the oldest building on the property, but it was her home with her daughter. Her home, her job. Gone in a phone call, without warning. She had taken several steps towards us, head down, and the trauma that I saw in her physical being was something I had never seen before in my lifetime. She was falling within herself. The breakdown was mental, emotional, and physical. I believed the next phone call we would be making would be for a medical emergency.

I grabbed an office chair with wheels and swept it behind her. "Sit down, Beverly. Sit down," I said gently, but firmly. "You're okay. You hear me? You're okay. We're here with you." The other girls became women then. They came, moving around her, consoling her with steady voices.

I took Carlie's arm and led her away. "Look, if Beverly doesn't calm down quickly, you will be calling the Medical Centre. She's hyperventilating, or worse. I don't know anything about medical stuff, but I'm telling you, she's going over the edge. You hear me?" I could feel the anger towards Donald growing in me. He was thousands of miles away and doing this shit.

Beverly stabilized before my deadline. We comforted her with compassion, and finally our words started to ring through to her.

We condemned Donald, as women will do when one of us is attacked. There is no wrath greater than a woman in moments like these. And all of us, at that moment, felt hatred towards Donald.

The brightest of the young reservation clerks, Lisa, forcibly defended Beverly. "I couldn't have done anything different than you, Beverly. Donald is a piece of shit for what he's done to you." Lisa had an education, had a college degree, and was working at the resort because her husband had taken a position at the police station for a portion of his remote training.

Beverly's residence allowed Donald to abuse her, to take advantage of her. Donald frequently took the liberty of asking her to go next door to the office to check the reservation bookings if he happened to be trying to book something late at night or early from the sports shows. He controlled her life, knew her vulnerabilities. He finally got her just to take the reservation books home with her. Rather than be sensitive to her life challenges, he used her. He had been slighted by a CEO, and he was mad. That rage was channeled to someone he could hurt, who was defenseless.

I was infuriated. Once again, I took Carlie aside. Her title was Reservation Manager in the winter. And this was clearly something she needed to manage. "You talk to *Don*," I said. "You tell him that he's kicking a single mom out on the street. You tell him, Carlie!" I breathed low and shallow. "Look, he can fire whoever he wants. But it's your responsibility to make it halfway decent. She has nowhere to go."

Carlie was solemn. As much as she did not want to talk to him, she saw the consequences for her. Donald might be the boss, but her happiness at work was in the few people left around her for the winter. She was ultimately responsible for the staff in the reservations department. We all knew it. If Beverly was going to be put out on the street, the remaining staff, including myself, would become both the jury and the judge of Carlie's lack of duty and compassion. She appeared somber and at the same time fearful, wide-eyed, unconsciously rubbing her stomach with the palm of her hand. All she could manage to say was, "Wish me luck," as she reluctantly made her way into Donald's office. We had managed to take Beverly next door and sit her in front of her television, wrapped in a blanket. She had a prescription for her nerves and we gave her a prescribed dose and brought the remaining bottle to the office for fear that she would take too many. We would check in on her for the rest of the day. We quietly waited for Carlie to reappear.

The door opened. Her face was flushed and brooding. "He was just joking with Beverly. Knows how to crank her up. She's not fired. I'm to tell her. It was just a prank."

"What an asshole," Brenda, the other reservation clerk, spoke up.

I shook my head. Not in disbelief, but in disgust. He found someone that was weaker. Someone that he could hurt, like he was hurt. He was full of revenge. Carlie had gotten his attention. She must have spelled it out, although I am not sure what she had to sacrifice.

I imagine most psychologists would connect narcissists back to their troubling childhoods. Maybe Donald had a troubling childhood. Maybe not. Maybe he'd been told that he was fat and ugly when he was a kid, and just never got over it. He could be charming, playful, and at times it was almost believable that he really cared. It was easy to want to see goodness and deny the intricate trappings. It was the single strand of the spider web from my past that would attach every once and awhile. I wanted to believe. I didn't want to see the ugliness. But the ugliness was always there, always reminding me like the foul smell of something rotting. It was practically invisible to the naked eye, not to the other senses.

We all needed him for employment, some more than others. Our choice to live in the pristine, beautiful, and remote north was blemished. Its beauty was hindered by our need for livelihood and tarnished and scarred by a monster.

None of us would forget this day. It was a turning point. I could see it in everyone, including Carlie. We would act no differently towards him than we ever did, but we would never forget, and never forgive.

CHAPTER 35

BRIAN

It was the first week of December. Snow fell and then melted during the day. The ice that formed in shallow bays softened and refroze. I would break through the ice with the boat. It split into large polished sheets that would stack on each other, with nowhere else to go. I left work at four p.m., and the last rays of light had already disappeared on the horizon by the time I arrived home. I would continue boating to work as long as I could.

The frost was heavy on the windshield on the boat in the boathouse that morning. It had been cold overnight, dipping as low as -4°F. A wind from the northwest curled around the boathouse entrance, encouraging me to scrape the windshield faster. Once in the boat and reaching the end of the big island, I knew I was in for a nasty ride. A northwesterly had blown in choppy waves that spewed into the boat as I quartered through it. Having lost the sapphire blue hue of summer, the lake was now pewter grey, menacing nimbostratus hanging above, replacing the fluffy cumulus backdrop on blue skies. It had been clear overnight, producing this cold temperature, but now the wind and clouds indicated a storm was brewing.

Each wave that quartered the boat threw large, heavy droplets on the windshield that instantly attached and froze. Most of it was on the passenger side. Layers of ice were building up that obstructed my view through the glass. Enough was being deposited on the driver's side that I eventually gave in, opening my front cover so that I could stand upright above the windshield. I shivered from the force of the northwesterly wind combined with the boat's speed.

As I reached the marina's dock and bay, I saw that the ice had tripled its perimeter from the day before. It ran the full distance of the bay's width, from point to point, encompassing the whole bay. This was likely my last trip in, unless the weather warmed, which was not common at this time of year.

As usual, I was off step, slowly penetrating forward so that the ice parted, giving room for the prop to spin uninhibited. The ice became thicker as I got closer to the dock. I was riding the bow up onto it, allowing the sheer weight of the front of the boat to break the ice that was now at minimum a half inch thick. I looked back and watched the big, clear sheets settle back into the water behind me. I was trapped. Sandwiched, like a tanker in the Arctic.

The ice had become too thick to break. If I reversed, I would shred my prop. I needed enough room to turn around. That is what paddles are for. With the boat in neutral, I worked one side of the boat to the other, pushing against the broken ice pieces, lifting smaller ones with the paddle, toppling them onto others to make room. I was moving the boat and ice inches at a time to turn the boat around. Once turned, I cleared as much ice as possible around the prop and made my way out of the bay. I had one more option. One more bay that was a bit further north, the water a bit deeper, with a suitable ramp that would allow for the removal of the boat for winter storage. I sent my usual prayer to the heavens and returned to open waters. I could tell instantly as I headed into the next bay that the freezing temperatures had less effect in the deeper water. The ice formation was half the area of the previous bay. I made it to the dock. This would be the last time I would see open water in the bay until spring. We had pre-arranged to have a local take me back to the island on his windjammer.

There was not much point in keeping the boat in the water any longer. We had made our way to Winnipeg over the course of the fall and purchased dry goods enough to last three months. A little longer than necessary, but always anticipating changes to Mother Nature's plans. Propane bottles were full, and even the old Servel refrigerator had been replaced with a smaller, more efficient propane model.

I used my marine radio to call the resort and signaled that I was officially on holidays until sometime after Christmas, or at least until I had two inches of solid ice to walk or ski the distance to mainland. Donald did not particularly care, as I had agreed to take the time off without pay. Everything was pre-arranged and planned. Carlie called my ride home, and I waited.

I did not wait long. I heard him from a long way. The windjammer is a flat bottom boat that glides over ice and water with an aircraft engine and propeller at the rear. The engine has a distinctive roar. Our only communication had been by telephone from the resort, and he had told me what to wear. I had prepped the boat for this occasion. I came equipped with ear protection, a full balaclava for my face, and a snowmobile bodysuit. It would be an open ride, with cold enough temperatures for severe frostbite.

I did not know what to expect. When I saw him enter the bay, I recognized the type of boat. It was like a boat that they use in the Everglades. Exactly like that, except it was much smaller, and Brian sat on a bench just below the wooden sides of the boat. Let me repeat, wooden. The sides were about sixteen inches high. It was not made for waves, and I deduced we would not be following a path that led us through the open waters of Whitefish Bay.

Brian skillfully slid the boat sideways onto the shore on solid ice. There was no verbal communication. The engine was too loud. He pointed to my seat, also a bench, but I could see that he wanted me to sit on the opposite side to balance our weight. He was a small man, wearing an aviator style hat with leather ear flaps. His face was bare, but I could see a piece of fabric below his weathered coat that he could pull up to cover his face. I knew in an instant that I liked this man. That smile was genuine, filled with gentle warmth and acceptance. His eyes spoke volumes. Dark brown iris, perfectly round, and I wondered if he had Metis or aboriginal background. His eyes reflected depth and wisdom and happiness. In an instant, I trusted this man for the ride.

Then I was on the ride.

It was not Brian that I did not trust. My hands clasped firmly to the side of the wooden boat; my feet planted to its floor. I watched the floor board quiver as he maneuvered it from water to ice. I watched it strain to stay intact. Beneath its wooden surface were two smooth runners that would guide the boat forward on solid ice—providing they stayed attached. The biggest expanse of open water was under the bridge where the current ran the strongest. I gripped the wooden side firmly as Brian sped up to make the transition. We cleared the open water under the bridge and were up on ice. I looked back at Brian, and with total respect and gratefulness gave him a thumbs up. I could see and feel his concentration on the craft as the wind pushed us sideways towards the shore. The boat had become a purple toboggan.

Brian carefully picked his way towards our island. He never came close to open water after the bridge. He stayed clear of the big waters that still hung in resistance in Whitefish Bay and chose a path winding its way north through a series of islands that led us from depths, away from open waters. When we emerged near our island, he had no choice. That morning I had crossed open water. Our island was now encapsulated with ice but too fragile to hold the weight of the windjammer. He tried to stay clear of the granite shore and made a run towards our dock. On the first attempt, he shattered the newly formed ice and veered away from shore, pushed by wind and building blocks of ice that formed as the boat broke through. I practically jumped to shore as home reached out to me, but then we were making a wide circle, the small boat shivering under the strain of shattering the recently frozen ice shield. We came up short once more, and Brian made another attempt to overcome the newly formed ridge that he had created, to get me close enough to depart. On the third attempt, he bridged the gap. He nudged the granite shoreline and I quickly threw my pack and grasped Jim's extended hand. I was home. The engine roared as he gave himself full throttle to cover the open water that he had created. The little wooden boat was up on solid ice again and sped away.

CHAPTER 36

THE GIFT

The clear night disappeared. We heard it come, the howling north-westerly. By morning, snow had already accumulated a couple of inches and with driving force was rapidly delivering more. It was too cold to be moist snow, and so it was carried with gale winds angling almost parallel with the shoreline. Visibility was poor. I felt blessed that we were safe, inside with the PIG started, the big heater freshly filled with birch.

We observed the changing landscape from the front room. We had only removed a portion of the polystyrene panels that provided an additional layer of insulation to the windows. Sekima was already outside, sleeping at the back door, protected from the wind, letting snow build steadily on his winter coat.

Jim was the first to see it. "Well, would you look at that," he said excitedly. He pointed towards the boathouse.

"What?" I could not believe it. Not ten feet from the corner of the boathouse, a large white-tailed buck was making his way across the ice parallel to our shoreline.

"He's got to be in rut," Jim said. "He's not even travelling upwind. Get Sekima in quietly. I'm getting my 270. I've got a good shot if he doesn't get spooked."

I scurried to the door, raising the inside door latch so that the click was barely audible. "Sekima," I said in a hushed tone. "Come here."

He looked up at me with half-closed eyes. I snapped my fingers which was a "come" command at close range. He rose slowly and shook, ridding himself of the accumulated snow on his back. As soon as he was within range, I grabbed his collar, not chancing a change of heart. I had him inside, and the door closed softly behind me.

Jim already had his boots on and the 270 shouldered.

"Is he still there?" I asked.

"He's past my line of sight from inside. I don't know, but I guess I'll find out soon enough." He gently raised the door latch, and I closed the door quietly behind him.

I held my breath, knowing that if he had the shot, he would not waste time. The buck had passed our visual range and I dared not remove the insulation from the other windows. The shot rang out sharply, silencing the northwesterly for one split second. One shot. I counted the seconds. Fifteen seconds. The door opened.

"He's down. Dropped immediately."

"Good shot, sweetie! All this time hunting this fall, and nothing."

"Delivered right to our doorstep. But now how do we get him?" Jim set his rifle down in a corner, took his coffee mug from the table and gulped down the remains.

He was right. That side of the shoreline had been open just two days ago. We'd had increasingly colder temperatures, but as of yet had not dared to test the ice under our weight.

"That buck probably weighs more than either of us, but he had weight distribution over four legs, not two."

"I guess I'm the one for the test." I laughed.

"It sure looks that way." Jim nodded.

"I wasn't being serious," I said nervously.

"Well, I am. I'll tie a rope to you. If you get out to him, you'll already know that the ice is safe for you to come back. You can tie the rope around his horns and I can pull him to shore."

"What if I fall in?"

"It will be cold." He smiled tenderly. "You'll be wearing a life-jacket and a rope. Trust me."

"Let's get it done before I lose my nerve." I knew Jim would never put me in harm's way. He'd likely made the same calculation as I had. The buck would be close to twice my weight, and it had fallen, hitting the ice with significant force.

It took some time to get ourselves rigged and discuss some of the details. If the ice cracked at all, I was to retreat. If it started to break, I was to lie prone. If I fell in, I was to make sure that I did not go under the ice. We went through it several times, and then headed out. Sekima was left inside as he would no doubt be on the buck before anyone, and yet another distraction.

I gingerly made my way onto the ice. I thought light. I made small steps. I was halfway there and feeling more relaxed.

"How are you doing?" Jim shouted from shore.

I waved back at him and gave him a thumbs up. The buck was a good fifty to seventy-five feet from shore, or so we had estimated. Our rope was a hundred feet long. I hoped we had enough.

I was close enough to now see the buck clearly. He was a five by five, big, sprawling antlers, thick neck from the rut. He was huge.

"He's the size of a cow!" I shouted to Jim. He had to weigh over two hundred pounds. I hesitated to get any closer, in anticipation that the added weight on the ice would give way. I saw no signs of cracking ice, but it gave me no comfort. This was the critical moment.

"Slide the looped end of the rope over his antlers." He yelled.

"I'm afraid if I get close to him the ice will crack."

I was close enough now that I could touch him. He was magnificent, brawny greyish coat, his eyes still wide. It always made me feel a bit sad, but I also believed he offered himself to us, a blessing. I listened intently for any signs that the ice was giving away. The snow had stopped and the day was clearing. The westerly wind had diminished to a cold breeze in my face. I heard nothing. I was on all fours, slipping the secondary rope over his antlers. There, I did it. I secured the rope around both sides of his antlers.

"Okay, I got it. Just a minute." I was much faster to retreat and hastily made my way back over the ice towards Jim.

"Jim, he is huge. I'm serious." I stepped onto solid ground.

He handed me the last few feet of the rope. He in front.

"On three. One, two, three."

We pulled. I could see the neck of the deer bend, but its body did not budge.

"Okay, again. One, two, three." I had tucked the rope behind my back and used my body weight. The deer remained motionless.

"What's going on?" I asked.

"It's too far away. We don't have the leverage we need from here."

"Now what?"

Jim looked up and down the shoreline as though the answer lay there. Perhaps a winch would be nice if we had a winch, or power.

"I have to get out there to pull it in."

"No way." I shook my head. "I won't be able to pull you out if you fall through."

"I don't intend on you pulling me out. I'll wear a life jacket. I'll take the canoe out. If the ice gives, I'll jump into the canoe."

"Really?" I asked in disbelief.

"Really," he said with conviction.

We worked the aluminum canoe down the snowy bank of the island and onto the ice. Jim set forth with the canoe in tow beside him. It was not easy, and it took him ten minutes to travel some fifty feet to where the deer lay. But he had not broken through, and I was relieved. Now came the difficult part.

With the canoe on one side, and the buck on the other, Jim strained to move the large animal. The deer's enlarged neck swiveled and his body moved several inches. The deer had not been walking towards our shore, but away from it, and it was necessary for Jim to turn his body completely if he was going to be able to pull. It had been part of the reason we were unsuccessful pulling from shore. Several more attempts, and Jim had the deer turned. Again, he strained, the rope around his midriff and held tightly in his left hand. He gained a couple of feet. He turned to the other side moving the canoe an equal distance.

I stepped off shore and came out some twenty feet towards them. "Should I pull on the rope too?" I shouted.

"No," he replied firmly.

Again, he took a secure stand, leaning forward. The deer moved several inches. I knew Jim would overcome any obstacle. Dragging the deer flatly over the surface showed little result. It could not be done that way in the bush, and it certainly was not any different on the snow-covered ice surface. Jim turned, walked over to the deer, removed the rope. He grabbed it by the antlers and hauled upwards and forwards. He kept moving forward and gained ten feet before he stopped. His other hand remained on the canoe, forwarding it at the same time. I could see him bent over, resting his hands on his knees, taking a break from his rigorous effort. The deer weighed as much as he did. Moments later, I watched as he took another grip on the antlers and strained forward. His boots caught slippery ice below and he collapsed, letting his grip on the antlers fall away. I heard the thump, the crash as he hit hard. I listened for the splinters, the cracking of the recently formed ice. It held.

It was nightfall before Jim had the deer dressed and hung by post and pulley in the boathouse. Sekima had claimed four deer legs and hooves from knee down. Because of the brutally cold temperatures, Jim had skinned the animal before it was no longer possible to remove the hide. For now, the entrails and skin were packed away in a plastic bag in the loft portion of the boathouse so that we did not attract prey overnight. We would deliver them to the neighboring island tomorrow and share our gift with wolves, fox, and birds of prey. We thanked the great buck. A gift had been delivered.

CHAPTER 37

DON'T GO WHERE
YOU DON'T KNOW

We waited for morning when the worst of the night's cold had passed. It was a pretty sight. The deep green of the evergreen forest, each tree branch dolloped with snow, bending the branches ever so slightly downward. The snow was fresh and unsoiled, the brightest white that made your eyes squint as the sun bounced reflections from the spotless crystal surface. It was not going to warm much this day, as temperatures overnight had dipped to -13°F and hovered at -4°F at ten a.m. Our daily chores would be interrupted by a trip to Channel to share the remains of the deer. Again, we left Sekima inside so that he would not follow us to the other island. He would not be seeing the outdoors today unless under strict supervision. Overnight should give ample time for the remains to be devoured.

The hanging meat had not yet frozen, protected from temperatures by the boathouse and its dissipating body heat. Although it was preferable to hang the meat three to five days, we would have to cut and wrap it later today before it was completely frozen solid. That in itself would take a few hours.

We left the boathouse on the ice, still following the shoreline. Jim was some twenty feet in front of me, carrying the bag of guts

180

and hide. It was so sudden. I had no time to scream. The ice gave way, and Jim disappeared below the surface into a blackened hole. In another instant, he porpoised his torso out onto ice that cracked but stayed intact.

"I'll get a rope," I yelled. "Hang on."

He did not answer me. He had lifted his torso onto the ice, throwing his body forward away from the open hole he had escaped. He was quick to his feet. I remained helpless to know what to do aside from not moving towards him. The plastic bag lay several feet away from the hole.

"Which way is shore?" he cried out. "I can't see."

"Head towards my voice." I quickly scrambled along the rocky shoreline towards a spot that was least treacherous. He stumbled, hands on the ground until he found some level footing.

I was ahead of him. "This way. You're on the path to the cabin. There's nothing in your way." I rambled, using my voice to guide him. "We're at the cabin door. I'm opening it."

"Okay." He rushed past me.

I ran towards the bed and grabbed the down comforter. By the time I came back, he had torn his boots and frozen clothes off; they were brittle and stiff. He stood there naked, violently shaking. The ice was already melting from his eyelids and eyelashes, running like tear drops down his face. Distraught from our sense of urgency, Sekima was at his side, licking his knees.

It took several hours before he felt warm again. Enough time for numerous hot chocolate drinks and for us to reason why the ice had given way so unexpectedly. The day before, we'd been further from shore and with much more weight with the big buck. That was the west shore. Jim fell through on the north side. The side that Brian had broken and busted with the windjammer. It was the only reason. It had somehow created a weakness in the ice, perhaps an air pocket at that very spot.

Jim was fortunate, and as usual his survival instincts were spot on. When he fell through, he stayed upright. When he hit the bottom of the lake, some fifteen feet down, he allowed his knees to bend and kicked off as hard as he could. It was enough to propel himself out. It was another of nature's lessons. We had another motto: "Don't go where you don't know." It would serve us well over the years.

CHAPTER 38

PACK MENTALITY

With depths of over two hundred feet, the central portion of Whitefish Bay fought the freezing temperatures and hung in a state of resistance to the bitter cold. Each morning we watched a great expanse of misty haze rise over the open breadth of water. Each day it shrank a little in size and we knew there would soon be an ending to that fluid body. We would no longer delight in the gentle lapping against our shoreline, and at the same time, we would no longer battle towering waves. She would be gone, deep in sleep, healing from human pollution until she was prepared to birth again.

Sekima's coat was stunning, his insulated undercoat allowing him to lie comfortably in the snow, nose tucked under his dense downy tail. His mane extended around his shoulders, giving him a stately lion quality. His color was a blend of browns and greys, each guard hair tipped in black. It was his season and his domain. His territory now extended to the horizon, where frozen snow and ice met the backdrop of blackened spruce and stately pine. When he was not napping in a snow bed, he was perched on our island, wary of intruders. From high up on the rock, he could examine any movement. He could be down the embankment in a heartbeat and although he could not catch up to deer, other prey may not be so fortunate.

The Pack was never far apart. How could we be, on a five-acre island? I enjoyed this time we had together, away from the mayhem at the resort, away from the petty arguments, away from the drama, away from the chauvinism of privileged men. If there was one thing Jim was not, it was chauvinistic or prejudiced. He had great respect for women. He always encouraged me to strive to achieve more from life, whether it be business or pleasure. He made love to me with both passion and tenderness. He never took. He always gave. He deplored men who made sexist comments, even men who referred to their girlfriends or wives as "her." He always referenced me with pride and esteem. Perhaps it was for that reason that he disliked Donald the most.

There would be new seasonal staff hired each year at the resort. Donald bestowed praise and encouragement, not for talent or intelligence, but for tight-fitting and revealing clothing, for girlish giggles at his attempts to be playful. Carlie was part of the culture. Hers was the responsibility of hiring seasonal staff. Most were blonde. Most had curvy figures. Most were innocent and receptive to Donald's subtle sexual encouragement. Carlie would hire the brightest of young men to work at the dock or guest services, but the young women had a remarkably different set of criteria, with significantly less education and experience than their counterparts.

My mind drifted back to the present moment. Here on the island, the tranquility, the pristine, pure truth of life. The unadulterated, unique and random formation of land, water and sky. The echo of your own thoughts and deeds with no distraction, no disruption, no diversion. I laughed at my philosophical moment. No distraction, of course, other than nature, who threw plenty of distractions our way.

Nature was pure truth, something that could not be fabricated or manipulated to fashion itself after something you wanted or believed. No matter how complex or basic, nature would not bend to human desires. It did not discriminate. It did not treat fairly, or justly, or unjustly. It did not favor, or seek approval. If you chose to be involved in nature, then it was wise to choose the best tools to deal with her ever-changeability. Her disguises were many, and like the Perfect Storm off the East Coast in 1991, she could take the most experienced, the most equipped. She could flatten cities and farmland, destroy forests and coastal waters. She could build brilliant sunrises and sunsets, bless crops with sunshine and nourishment from the skies, feed all creatures, including the human race. She spoke in pure truth and did not compromise. She spoke constantly and fervently, if we were equipped to listen.

Within nature, there could be no denial of your fate. If you did not have enough wood for winter, you could blame it on a terribly cold winter, but there was no way to deny the truth of cold that permeated through to your inner core. If you somehow rationalized that it would get better in a month or so, well, maybe that was long enough—then again, maybe it was not. No good could come from denying your fear. The only thought or emotion that was worthy of observation was fear itself. And it was simple. Is this life threatening or not? If it is, what resources do I have to overcome the threat?

Jim bellowed. I laid my snow shovel down and ran. I looked out towards the boathouse where I had heard the yell from. His booming voice always meant trouble. There he was, making his way across the stretch of ice and snow that extended towards Barney's Narrow. I could see that he had in hand his large axe that he used for splitting wood. Beyond, I could see Sekima and a long black animal, low to the ice. It had to be an otter. It was far longer than Sekima. I could see that it wanted nothing to do with the dog. Its short front legs, and even its smaller rear legs, gave it an awkward waddling look as it moved forward. Sekima was cautiously taking up at its rear, pushing the animal along by his presence, but staying clear of a confrontation.

The animal would be ferocious in a fight with Sekima. It would be largely protected by its insulated thick, fatty pelt, heavily muscled and adaptive to both land and water. A relative of the weasel, it had a full mouth of sharp teeth for eating fish and even small animals. It no doubt was trying to make it back to a hole in the ice, and had been veered off course by Sekima's pursuit. I was certain that Jim carried the axe to assist the otter's efforts in returning to the water and avoid a battle that would no doubt cause serious injury to both dog and otter.

Jim's presence did not help reduce the conflict. Sekima now had Pack help. As Jim got nearer, Sekima became more aggressive and more confident. He wove from side to side of the otter, driving forward, occasionally snapping at its rear. Suddenly, the otter turned. It was too close to the shore, nowhere to go, and turned to fight. It lunged at Sekima, using its powerful torso to come to the dog's height. It swiveled its vertebrae from side to side, making ready to find a killing spot. It lacked the speed. With one swift drive, Sekima charged, jaws snapping shut on the side of its neck. Sekima swung his head side to side; with quick sweeps of his powerful neck, he snapped and shattered the otter's vertebrae and dropped him dead on the ice.

There was no choice but to dispose of the otter down its own hole, as the big malamute wanted the kill for his own. Like his ancestors, he killed by instinct, but had not been driven by hunger. He was driven by curiosity and the Pack mentality.

There are so many comparisons to Pack mentality in humans, but so deliberate and cruel to make this incident seem like child's play. The bully that uses his size and influence to control others, gathers the support of others that feed off his power and control. Until they, too, are willing to do the horrific. Carefully surrounding the weaker, prodding and pushing, snapping and gnawing, wounding and going in for the kill. Collectively forming a political Pack, lying, cheating, spreading false information, destroying a person and their family for personal gain. Stripping them of dignity and life resources.

Over and over, the rich denying and rationalizing that the poor had a choice over their life circumstances, and the worst rationalization of all, that their control and power had nothing to do with any of it. A Pack with incredible power. A Pack of Christians that killed and maimed Indigenous people because they believed they had the right as a superior race. A Pack of white. A Pack of black. A Pack of any collective to protect its beliefs or survival, with instinct to kill, and a human mind to rationalize the kill for any purpose.

A domesticated animal. No need to kill. No need to eat. An instinct to hunt. Pressed to kill for survival. Through our intervention, our whole Pack was responsible for the kill. We knew the wrong.

CHAPTER 39

PROMISE TO COME HOME

There was still time for one more hunt for white-tail deer before the season closed. The big buck was a blessing, and if we got one more, we would not be buying meat for a long time. Our deep freeze was a big one that required no electricity, with temperatures well below freezing. The deep waters of Whitefish were still open. We could see the rising fog in the middle, signaling open water. The ice was thick enough for us to walk on the north side of our island and down the long passageway called Barney's Narrows, which flanked the big island. There was a snow blanket of about three inches, pristine, untouched.

The day was bright and cold, no wind, perfect for being outside. The island was far too large to chase, but we did decide to segment a portion of it that we were familiar with, north of the bog. We had licensed Sekima, and although he was not trained, he would run circles around me, exploring the bush. It was enough to keep deer from sneaking behind me. Hopefully enough to keep them moving ahead towards where Jim would be sitting. That is, if there were any to be found.

We had carefully laid out our plan. In total, it would take approximately three hours. We had reviewed the navigational map and had decided that we would come out to the red buoy by three p.m. Jim left an hour before me so that he could be sitting and quiet long before I entered the bush. In the event that there was trouble, three rapid rifle shots, but if someone did not make it out before dark, the other would wait until morning. Jim made me promise. Survival of one was dependent on the other remaining clear of harm's way.

I was cautious of my footing. Snow in the bush could hide treacherous, uneven ground, or conceal loose rocks. Twisting an ankle, or falling and breaking a bone would lead to peril. We were, once again, on our own with no communication with the outside world. Have a plan. Stay alert. Stay safe.

Occasionally I would glimpse Sekima's wolf-grey coat between the gnarly jack pine. The crunch of snow underfoot prevented me from hearing him, although I suspected he made no sound. I had not seen any signs of deer. Their tracks would be evident, and by now if they were on this part of the island, they would have established a path. I found none. It was already two forty-five in the afternoon. Although I had not reached Jim's position, I needed to go to the shoreline as we had already arranged. I whistled and shouted for Sekima to follow as I picked a path leading to the lake.

I was pleased when I stepped onto the snow-covered ice. It was exactly three p.m., and off to my left shoulder was the red buoy. Perfect timing. Sekima bounded down the side of the island and trotted over to where I stood. I could see from north to south down the channel until the meandering passageway changed course. No sign of Jim yet. I had not heard any rifle shots that would indicate a deer kill. I played with Sekima for a while and finally sat down on a rock to give myself a break. I waited.

A half hour later, I was still waiting—no sign of Jim. Once again, fear was creeping in at the edges of my mind. The first signs of dusk were starting, shadows as the sun made its way to the horizon. I was not in danger, but I shot the rifle. Three shots in the air. Sekima retreated back into the bush, sensitive ears avoiding the deafening crack. I waited. Surely, he would hear me and respond to let me know where he was. Silence.

Close to four p.m. It would not be long before I was engulfed by dusk and then darkness. I was at least a half-hour walk from our cabin. I yelled into the air. My voice echoed back to me. There was that sickening, nauseating feeling again, from fear when it permeates through your consciousness.

I did not want to believe that something had happened to Jim. Had he fallen? It would have to be something of significant magnitude for him to stay in the bush. Was he unconscious—was that why he had not responded to my shots? I wanted so much to go back in the forest, find his tracks that would lead me to him. I had promised not to. I had to leave. I had to go now. I had to return to the cabin, stoke the fires for the night. And wait until morning.

As I got to the mouth of Barney's Narrows, Sekima ran off the point towards me. There was some comfort that he was with me. Our island lay dark against the sky, and I could make out the silhouette of the boathouse. As soon as I arrived, I found a flashlight and lit the coal oil lanterns, added wood to the fireplace, and wondered how I would survive the night with so much fear around me. I prayed. *Dear lord, please let him be safe. Please keep him safe throughout the night.* A tear escaped, and then another.

When there is nothing you can do in a situation, the powerlessness exposes how vulnerable and defenseless you really are to life itself. Perhaps it is the very reason that some people are born again, or turn to God, or some faith they had in their past. The human psyche must survive and it strives to create any conditions in order to do so.

I wondered what it would be like to have no hope. I was Metis. It meant my ancestors left the reservations with their native wives.

But what of those they left behind? The children that did not come home from the white man schools. Beaten by Christian priests and nuns, to death. Their parents' anguish. Their pain. Their hopelessness. And so, the eternal fire is tended for the spirits of those and others, for it is the only hope they had, and still do. Those souls, never forgotten.

Hope is paramount to creating an environment of strength, resolve, and problem solving. The psyche is ready for hope, willing to grasp at a thread if offered.

There had to be something I could do. I already knew I would start out at daybreak. I could prepare for that, food, water, blanket, bandages. But it was only five-thirty. The night ahead was dark and long. I could not stop thinking of what could have gone wrong. Perhaps he had been too far away to hear my shots. I had seen his footprints getting onto the island, but none returning. How could I have missed that? Where would I start to look? We had not discussed how far down Barney's Narrows he would travel.

I knew I could not look for him tonight, but I did not have to sit in the cabin and perhaps miss some sign of him being alive. The coat, the boots, the gloves, the flashlight, the gun, just in case. Sekima close on my heels. Even in the darkness, I could see the outline of the entrance to Barney's Narrows, blackened and framed by land on either side, clear sky and crescent moon. One more time. Raising the rifle, I shot three times in succession.

Within seconds, I heard the reply. Three rifle shots in succession. I was overwhelmed, tears streaming down my face. My God, he is alive and near. The shots were not far away. Sekima was down the bank and running. Nothing was going to stop me from leaving our island. I promised myself I would not go into the bush. I would stay on the channel. I could easily follow my tracks back. Sekima disappeared around the first bend. As I approached the turn, I made out the outline of dog and man steadily coming my way.

"Did you not see my fire?"

"What fire?"

He explained that when I had not come out, he'd lit a big fire on the ice. He had been waiting there since shortly after three.

"That's not possible. I was out at three, just like we planned."

It hit both of us at once. We had come out at three, but we were not at the same location. There were two navigational red buoys. I came out to the first, and Jim further north. The rifle shots did not carry to him, or were masked by the crackling fire that he had built.

Sekima ran big circles around us as we made our way back to the cabin. The night air had changed. We were caressed by the bitter cold, the brightness of the winter sky pregnant with stars, and gratitude for our safety. We had found each other once again.

CHAPTER 40

THRESHOLD

We had been discussing it for at least two weeks, and watching. Our friend was coming from Alberta to visit us for Christmas but we did not have enough ice to cross. Each day we would slip down to the shore and watch the progress of freeze-up. The ice had formed many weeks before between the islands, giving Sekima full freedom as he trotted across the three hundred yards to the island north of us. There was not a lot of snow. Still three inches or so that would not provide good insulation. We could get total freeze-up soon. If we could just get cold weather consistently below the -4°F mark, it would make plenty of ice. An inch a night. We needed three to walk. Three strong inches.

For now, the ice in the shallower depths of fifty to sixty feet had eventually formed, no longer able to hold off winter. It was four to six inches. But to the south of us, towards mainland, the big expanse of water resisted. With depths of over two hundred feet in the center, the lake simply would not succumb to ice. Every breath of the northerly winds would allow her ample movement to viciously break up any ice that tried to form. A luminous black hole encompassing over a mile of our path to mainland prevented us from crossing to town on foot.

Arrangements were made with Edie and Les, our good friends in town, to accommodate our friend until it was safe to travel across the lake. But as the dates on the calendar were checked off, it became clear that a decision would need to be made determining whether our friend would be able to join us for Christmas. Temperatures were to drop to below -6°F on the 20th of December and plummet to -17°F after Christmas. As we suspected, on December 20th the big waters gave way to old man winter. We could no longer see the black hole.

"It's going to stay at these temperatures and keep dropping. We are finally making ice!" I was excited.

"There's not enough to get Gayle out here."

"But if it continues like they say, we could possibly have her here for Christmas. We can walk at three inches."

We had many discussions about weather before the world took notice of weather. The most significant ruling factor to life on an island was weather, as much as politics in the city. Luckily, most of our decisions about weather conditions were favorable. Jim knew that I was right this time. We would make ice in the next few days. There were no guarantees that ice would form evenly and perfectly across every mile. The big hole had been the last to go, and although we could hug the shoreline, it did not guarantee our safety.

"We'd have to bar across the hole anyway." The needle bar, a heavy metal bar with a pointed end would be thrown ahead like an arrow. If it hit the ice and bounced off, it meant that there was enough to walk. If it penetrated and water appeared, it was unsafe.

"It's not like we haven't done that before."

We stood on the dock at the shoreline, the dark silhouette of pines against a dappling of cumulous clouds that hung low, with a blush of pink. Yesterday, steam had billowed from the open water as a last attempt to fight the long icy containment of winter. It appeared like a giant white cloud rising as high as a twenty-storey building. It caused a layer of shoreline frost that jewelled the brittle branches of deciduous trees and built encasements around the evergreen needles like hornet nests. Winter had as many magnificent scenes as any other season.

"It would be reassuring to wear a life jacket, but it wouldn't do much good when the water is barely above freezing," Jim said.

"We have wet suits. If we fell in wouldn't that provide insulation?" I offered.

"It's probably not a bad idea. It would likely provide enough time to at least get out of the water before hypothermia sets in."

Our discussions were commonly like this. It made us a good pair. Determined to solve a problem, one of us would suggest a remote possibility or hypothetical situation. The other would latch onto the idea, and so on, and so on, until we had devised a realistic plan—or so we thought. Wearing wetsuits across the recently frozen expanse was just the edge we were looking for.

We tested our theory by suiting up. We not only found the wetsuits comfortable, but we were also quite warm as the suits insulated us from the wind. Without hesitation, we prepared our packs and remaining emergency kit for the walk into town. We knew that if we made it without falling in, then our travel back with our friend would be the same.

Wearing full bodysuits of neoprene and light winter jackets, we harnessed ourselves together by a stretch of heavy nylon rope, approximately twenty feet. The rope would be our safety guard if one of us fell in. The other would have to quickly react by locking to the ice with ice picks we carried, to prevent being pulled in by the other. The ice picks were designed to dig into the ice, which would hopefully provide enough leverage until the person who fell in was able to get out. The rope that tied us together would serve two purposes. If one of us fell in, it could be very difficult to get out of the water. Hauling body weight with wet clothes, a pack, and heavy winter boots, using only your arms, would be challenging enough. Add the slippery, wet, and likely breaking surface of ice to crawl onto, and we would be faced with an extremely difficult task. The person who fell in could be helped by the other pulling on the rope. It was not likely that I would be able to pull Jim, who was close to twice my weight, but any assistance might be enough to save his life.

The second and less obvious reason for the rope was related to the dynamics of breaking through ice on a lake. When the ice breaks under your weight, gravity immediately pulls you under. Until you have a chance to swim and use your body's buoyancy to bring you up, you are freefalling downwards. Assuming you are conscious and fighting to the surface, when you finally do emerge you may very well be some distance from the hole you went down. You are now trapped under the ice unable to break through, as difficult as trying to break a balloon from the inside out. Worse yet, the darkness that surrounds you destroys any visual recognition of the hole you came down. It is merely by chance that you would find your way to the exact spot you broke through. The rope acts as a path back to the surface where you entered. Jim had been in shallow depths when he had fallen through before. But these were the big waters.

We set off that morning, on December 23rd, encouraged that it had been -6°F the night before, and holding temperatures of 2°F that morning. Jim was in the lead with the seven-foot metal bar by his side. I held back, almost fifteen feet behind him. He used the bar to determine the ice thickness twice in the first quarter mile. He was certain it would not be necessary again until we came close to the where the open water had resisted the longest. Having only recently frozen, it had not accumulated the snow cover like the rest of the lake. A light flurry had whitened its appearance, and it was distinctive in its visible hollow shadow appearance.

"Hold up. I need a break," I called.

Jim stopped and waited for me to come closer. I maintained a short distance.

"I'm really having a difficult time in this suit. The inside of my thighs is burning something brutal. How about you?"

"I'd have to say the same. There's no give in these suits."

"It's terrible. I seriously don't know if I can walk the distance. We haven't gone a quarter of the way."

"You wanted to do this. If we had waited a few more days we wouldn't have to be subjecting ourselves to this." He was quick to remind me why we had made this choice to prematurely cross the lake. He wanted me to find the resilience I would need if we were going to continue. I was replaying a track from last winter.

"Okay. Let's move on," I said half-heartedly.

"We can stop lots along the way. Just let me know if you want to take a break." I could see the same exhaustion in his face, but he would not stop. We were committed.

We had walked another few hundred yards when I pulled on the nylon rope that connected us. Jim looked back to see me lying on the ice and snow. He reluctantly walked back to where I lay.

"I swear I can't make it another hundred yards, let alone a couple of miles."

Seeing the painful look on my face, he responded tenderly. "Do you want to go back?"

"I don't know." I fought back tears. "This wetsuit is like wearing a condom around your body." I laughed at my own analogy.

Jim laughed with me. Extending a hand, he helped me back to my feet. He gave me a hug.

"It will get better. You haven't crossed your pain threshold yet," he said encouragingly.

"And why would I want to? That sounds ridiculous."

He explained to me about hitting the wall. At the last moment, when your muscles are in complete pain, and you do not think you can take another step, you must control all negative thoughts. It will pass and you will find that on the other side, there is relief.

Adrenaline kicks in, and you can go for miles more.

Over an hour later, we found ourselves on mainland. Gratefully, we had found our biggest hurdle was endurance from wearing the wetsuits—which were to prevent death should we fall into the icy waters of Lake of the Woods in December. We had our truck on mainland and didn't bother taking the suits off until we got to Edie and Les'. They gave us dry towels. Our suits were soaked wet with perspiration. Our outlook improved. We would walk back that afternoon, following our footsteps, Gayle in tow, and our rubber resistance suits in a pack.

"Ohhh, my kids. Look at this beauty." Gayle squealed her delight. Gayle was really only a few years older than Jim, but she fondly referred to us as kids. I had met her years prior, before I met Jim. When she did meet Jim, they were instantly bonded by their background in art. She was tirelessly up for an adventure at Lake of the Woods, so long as we told her it was safe to do so. She gave no thought to the danger of crossing the lake with so little ice.

"So, you think if I follow these tracks in the snow here, my fat butt won't fall in?" she laughed contagiously. She was indeed overweight, but at five-foot-eleven, she was no small woman, and her carriage was proud and tall. She had been ferociously attacked most of her life by inflammation of various sorts, and the latest hip replacement was not going to stop her.

The Canadian winter wilderness was uplifting. Gayle's innocence with nature and pure pleasure boosted our tired bodies as we made our way across the white expanse. The vast flat stretch of white snow lay before us, unspoiled by anything but our tracks of that morning. The islands stood stately against the dazzling blue sky, dotted only with a few liquid clouds. There was no apprehension of the ice condition, or weather. The magic of nature united with the solidarity of friendship and triumphed over our weariness.

CHAPTER 41

CHRISTMAS

Back on the island for Christmas, we gave no thought to the ice conditions over the deep water. Our world was a remote bubble that encompassed not only the island but several miles of solid ice, a wasteland of connecting islands.

Any shopping for food and Christmas gifts had been done long before we had pulled our boat from the water. Winter gave us the luxury to use the outdoors as a freezer without having to power any appliance. The turkey had been pulled to thaw for Christmas. A last-minute Christmas wreath was assembled using spruce bows and twine, covered with gold-painted pine cones and red-painted pistachio nuts.

Outside, temperatures hovered at -6°F all of Christmas Day. The turkey cooked on a traditional charcoal Weber BBQ, holding Sekima spellbound for the day. His usual ramblings to a nearby island to check for unwary beavers were thwarted. By the time the golden-brown bird arrived in the kitchen, it was almost too much for Sekima to bear. Jim's famous gravy was liberally added to his dry dog food before we set to eating Christmas dinner.

The granite fireplace radiated heat towards the dining room, making the flames of white candles on the table tremble slightly. The original cabin, built in 1946, held a certain charm, like a comfortable, worn moccasin. Although we had fully insulated the exterior walls, which hid the log surface, the interior walls with open rafters remained honey-colored, and the original chinking material, like braided horse hair, remained intact. It might have been a similar scene some fifty years prior.

The table had been set with white linen, the best worn china, and my parents' set of silver cutlery. Large bowls of food practically covered the entire table. There was turkey and dressing, cabbage salad, fresh baked rolls, mashed potatoes and yams, and the usual condiments of homemade pickles and beets, cranberries, and plenty of gravy.

"Gayle, you will have some Chardonnay with dinner, won't you?" I asked.

"Yes, my dear. If I'm going for the whole lot, I might as well have wine too."

I finished pouring Gayle's glass and waited for Jim to decide. It was a rare occasion that Jim would have a glass of wine, and this was usually one of them.

"Sure." Jim had already dished a large drumstick onto his plate and passed the serving platter to Gayle.

"Can we say grace?" I did believe in thanking God for this bounty. Christmas to me was about the birth of Christ, the son of our Lord, who gave to us his only son. In many religions there existed the same mysterious wanderer, the same figure who had led us to believe in something more.

Jim put his fork down, looking longingly at the plate of food in front of him.

"Thank you, God, for this joyous day of Christ's birth, our food, our friendship, and our love that has brought us together."

"Amen," we said in unison.

Both Jim and I had been brought up as Christians, but we had slipped away from the Church. We didn't talk about it much, about our belief in God or Christ. Both of us grounded ourselves in nature, and as far as I knew, we both believed that nature was God's creation, and nature was our Church.

"Oh, Jim, this bird is delicious. Hmmmm." Gayle announced her pleasure.

"And done in half the time that it would take in the oven. Did I share that story of doing a thirty-pound bird in two-and-a-half hours?"

"No, I don't believe you did. Hmmmm." Gayle had just tasted the sweet potato.

Jim recited the story. He had offered to cook a turkey for a corporate party. It was the day before Thanksgiving. He kept having women come up to him, worried that he had not yet started the turkey.

"They had never tasted your awesome bird? Hmmmm." Gayle was indeed in love with her food.

"No. Well, they got so worried about it that some of them decided to go home and cook a turkey because they didn't believe me." Jim laughed as he poured additional gravy on his dressing.

"Hmmmm."

"Do you ever stay quiet when you eat?" Jim asked, slightly annoyed by Gayle's persistent delight with her tastebuds.

"No, not really. Not when it is this good."

"You mean, you do this at home all the time?" Jim questioned.

Gayle was as empty as we were at Christmas. A time of the year to be joyous had an underlying melancholy. There had been no reconciliation for Jim of any of his family, including his mother, estranged relationships with a brother and children. For me, my siblings had their own families, children and grandchildren while I had chosen to have no children. Gayle had a disappointing divorce, and children that were not aware, and too distant to comfort her. We were a funny lot in that we never would admit how vacant Christmas was, and how much we did not want it to be that way. It glued us together. Brought us happiness and comfort. Another Pack.

Gayle confided that the meals she and her mom made were very basic. Gayle had lived with her mom even when she'd been married. She was just one of those moms that you wanted around. At eighty-five, she still made her way to the recreation centre for swimming and yoga.

"So, you don't go around *hmmmm*ing on a regular basis?" Jim needled.

I gave him a look to suggest he should stop.

"I guess it must just be with your food. I don't really think about it. It just seems that it slips out of my mouth when I taste these delicious morsels. Hmmmmm," she said. "But if it bothers you, dear, I'll try to stop. I just don't know if I can."

It was exactly the way I wanted Christmas to be. There were handmade gifts, there was homemade food, there was peaceful joy between good friends, all blessed by the grace of God in an environment that isolated us from the troubles of the world.

Of course, Jim wasn't satisfied that Gayle could not stop her *hmmm*. He did not believe for a second she could not stop. They would come to this impasse many times in the years to come. Jim would try to change some behaviour he would judge as irritating, and Gayle would try for a bit to adjust. Most often, she would revert back to how she had done things, and most often, he would stop nagging at her to change. Over his lifetime, Gayle seemed to be the only person besides me that could get away with being herself.

Gayle was an artist. Like most of our close friends, she was unconventional. She would work with any medium, whether it was metal, wood, paper, glass, or even the odd large animal bone that we discovered in the bush and saved for her. She delighted in the multitude of textures that were readily available to the lake and the islands. They were far superior to the conventional retail stores. Over her short time after Christmas, armed with a mosaic of pictures that she brought to use for collages, she feverishly chose from Jim's wide selection of brushes and paints. They had very little else in common, but the tie that binds artists was evident.

They exchanged ideas about paint applications to produce distinctive results, interpretations of what they saw in the random but perfectly balanced landscapes, and shared creative aspirations of how to improve their work.

I watched them in envy and in gratitude.

CHAPTER 42

NEW YEAR'S

Most of the afternoon was spent cutting deadfall and gathering it on the huge, flat rock at the shoreline of the large Crown-owned island just north of our island. It was in preparation for our ceremonious bringing in of the New Year. It was a celebration that Gayle had not experienced. She was enchanted by the notion of having a bonfire out in the wilderness.

Temperatures had not risen since Gayle had arrived. In fact, they had plummeted as they usually did around this time of the year. Daytime was lingering around -6°F and New Year's Eve promised to be a whopping -36°F. Still, tradition was tradition on the island. I would prepare a Chinese dim sum, or an equally challenging cuisine for our remoteness, and at approximately eleven p.m. we would make our way to a spot that we knew would be sheltered from the wind. It was usually the island across from us, as it gave us protection from both northerly and northwesterly winds. The ice was still impassable to vehicles, and there was no reason for any snow machines to be out this way on the lake.

As with most city dwellers, Gayle was in no way prepared for spending more than ten minutes outside in these temperatures. She had already borrowed long underwear, socks, and flannel shirts from Jim, who made no mention of the fact that the long underwear would come back to him in a different shape than when given. Although critical of human annoyances that he believed were curable by a mere shift in behaviour, he was opposed to personal insult. It was one of the qualities that I admired.

The worn one-piece snowsuit, from a time when Jim was much bigger, was brought out of storage, as were the oversized snow boots with felt liners. Gayle's feet were two sizes larger than mine and a full five sizes smaller than Jim's. There was not much choice in the matter if she was going to partake in our New Year's celebration.

Several packs were loaded with more food and beverages, including a bottle of champagne. Folding lawn chairs were stacked on the purple toboggan with the packs. We each had our own flashlight, although it was quickly apparent that we did not need a light source. The moon shone as brilliantly as a floodlight, illuminating a black and white landscape. The winter portrait of unsoiled snow, with only a single path where we had walked earlier in the day, was easily visible. So was the distant shoreline feathered by the blackness of pines of various heights stretching into the pool of sapphire sky—yet another layer of magic. With no cloud cover, every star constellation common to the northern hemisphere and the Milky Way fought for presence in the heavens.

"Oh, my goodness!" Gayle shared her delight.

"Beautiful, isn't it?" I said.

We made our way across the picture frame in single file, not daring to fan out and lose the simple affect. Jim was in the lead, towing the toboggan, Sekima well ahead surveying the shoreline.

"Boy, these boots are a little strange to walk in." Gayle had worn her slippers inside the large snow boots and was having some difficulty balancing her frame.

"Gayle, the crotch of your snow suit is at your knees." I burst into laughter at the sight.

"Don't I know it." She laughed, mildly attempting to hoist the suit upwards on her body and stay balanced.

"You probably could be mistaken for a sasquatch."

"It's a wonder more of them aren't seen then because they can't be very light on their feet."

"Are you coming?" Jim was now far ahead of us.

"I should be there by midnight." Gayle snorted with amusement.

Jim waited patiently for us to reach the shore before dousing the prepared dry wood with kerosene that he had brought over in the afternoon. A single wooden match started the small teepee of wood. He quickly added larger pieces from the stack we had prepared. Sekima explored the shoreline, his wolf-like stature an impressive silhouette against the bank. With no wind, the fire crackled and grew to a height of ten feet or more, throwing sparks upwards into the sky. Gayle and I moved back from the blaze.

"Anyone want a chair?" Jim asked.

"I don't think so," I said. "Not until I've determined how hot this is going to get."

"Look!" Gayle squealed.

The fire blazed upwards into the sky, throwing streams of turquoise and greens amidst the vibrant golden hues. It danced and laughed in pulsating unison with its own breath.

"How's that for fireworks?" Jim was satisfied with the display.

"How did you do that, Jim? It's an amazing light show."

Having seen it many times before, I explained nature's gift. It was the sap from the jack pine trees. For some reason the resin was unlike that of any of the other pines. It gave off iridescent colours.

"Those poor city folks," Gayle exclaimed. "They just don't know what they're missing."

"Nature is clearly designed to satisfy even the basic needs of fireworks at New Year's." Jim threw another busted branch onto the existing blaze.

We sat at the edge of the fire, talking to Gayle about our life on the island so far. She did not quite understand how Jim, who she knew as being highly intellectual, would be satisfied with this simple existence. She was equally surprised that I seemed to blossom in this cold, harsh environment with so few people around me. She did not realize that a simple life in nature is not simple at all. It had become one of the most challenging things either of us had done, and one of the richest.

One thing she knew for certain: her friends were happy at their island home, and she found it hard to resist this place herself. We shared the salami, crackers, and cheese, including offerings to Sekima. We did not trust that he would not take off on his own New Year's rendezvous if we did not call him occasionally and offer some exquisite treat.

We prepared our champagne a few minutes before midnight. The plastic cork made a pop. Jim, always conscious of the environment, made a careful note where it landed so that we would not leave it behind. We had brought plastic cups for the occasion so that they could be burned in the fire after they were used. It was not elegant, but it served the purpose.

"Here's to new adventures to come."

"Here's to good friends and more island adventures." Gayle raised her glass.

"Here's to a bigger fire next year." Jim laughed.

Sekima stood sentinel as we all hugged. Jim and I kissed feverishly. Our lives were indeed rich.

The temperatures were plummeting, promising that -36°F would be reached sometime close to morning. The last half of the champagne was poured like a slushy into our glasses. Embers on the rock would glow long into the night as we dreamed of our good fortune.

In a few days, we would walk back to mainland and say our goodbyes, our friendship enriched by memories and connections never forgotten, always treasured.

Moments of favorable weather over the next few days allowed us to explore, in depth, the shorelines of neighboring islands, and cross-country ski. Gayle used the flat ice surface to strengthen her new hip, completing not one, but two complete circles daily around our island. Some people think the body will just automatically recover, come back to brand new when a part is replaced. We knew different. So did Gayle. If she was to walk straight, or walk at all, she would have to force herself to use that leg, walk upward with no bending of the back to relieve the pain. The pain would be intense, but she used the forces of nature to find strength in those moments.

CHAPTER 43

FAMOUS

The largest area of Whitefish Bay finally frozen, temperatures plummeting to -17°F, with highs of -6°F during the day. We had walked to mainland as early as possible, but yet we remained cautious.

Trout season had opened on January 1st. The deep, clean waters of Whitefish brought anglers from the United States. It was only a few days after we'd returned Gayle to mainland. We heard them before we saw them—a continuous drone and buzzing that pierced the silence. We were outside getting firewood, our weekly chore. It took a few hours as we filled a large utility area so the wood would thaw and be easier to burn.

The buzzing stopped and we made our way down to the dock. It would be helpful to know where they came from. The weight of their snow machines would require far more than the three inches we needed to ski.

"I should check it out," I said. "I'll just ski over and see where they came from."

"They will sure be surprised to see a pretty woman out here." Jim chuckled.

"No doubt. And what about Sekima?"

"A pretty woman with a wolf. Wow!"

I asked him if he wanted to go with me, but he held back, thinking it would be more fun to watch.

There had not been a lot of snow yet. Plus, the snow didn't accumulate on the ice like it did on the island. The term windswept is accurate. We had a nice bed of six inches of snow on the island, but out here on the flats of the lake, there did not appear to be much more than three.

I waited until I was within shouting distance.

"Hi, gentlemen." They had watched me approach, surprise written on their faces. There were five of them, each with their own snow machine, elaborate-looking things with sleds behind them. They had already used their ice augers and were setting up lines.

"Hello," several of them replied in unison.

"Where did you come from?" a man with a full beard and reddish curly hair asked.

"That island, right there. We live here all year round."

"You're kidding? Way out here."

I asked where they had come onto the lake, and how much ice they had coming out. They not only had identical snow machines, they were all wearing the same clothing, at least from chest down. All in heavy yellow pants with black bibs. All about the same weight and stature, different ages and faces.

"Most of it five inches, some places a little more."

"That's great. You're out trout fishing?"

They told me that they came to the same place every year shortly after opening and that they were from Minnesota. One of them was uncovering a video camera and tripod from a sled.

"Looks like you're ready to take in the action." I nodded at the fellow with the camera.

He chuckled. "Well, there's only one famous guy with us. That would be Sal over there." He dipped his head acknowledging one of the older men with a broad flat face framed by thick pepper-grey hair.

"I don't know too many famous people, especially one that's

trout fishing?" I let my question hang there.

"Hi. I'm from the Fisher Tales, Cal Jones." Cal walked over and shook my gloved hand, warily eyeing Sekima who could hardly contain his enthusiasm for new people.

"Please to meet you. I'm sorry, I don't watch many of the Sports Channels. This is Sekima. He's very friendly. I'm just keeping him on his lead because he would likely be jumping on all of you."

I had found out what I needed and took leave. We were gaining ice quickly. I would follow their snow machine tracks, far easier than walking in fresh snow.

Jim and I found the dock deck that faced the big island to be the spot of choice, for any season. It had the prettiest of sunrises and sunsets and was well protected from the north winds. Our binoculars were always handy as we viewed a soaring eagle or a white-tail come to the water's edge on the big island. As we sipped on hot chocolate late that afternoon, we discovered the reason for the matching apparel. Excited tones alerted us that the men had caught a trout. What we then saw was the filming, Cal slipping in for the final shot as the trout was pulled from the hole. Obviously, the film would be edited to appear that Cal had done all the catching.

The lake's attraction never ceased to amaze us. From Goldie Hawn and Kirk Russell to the Rothmans, who built their empire on cigarettes, the beauty and the abundance on the lake was magic to those that experienced her. Most were ill-equipped to challenge her power, but some tried.

CHAPTER 44

INFAMOUS

Not so famous, but perhaps infamous, was Paul, who had built us an ice road, spanning one hundred feet wide. We were grateful to come and go as we pleased, similar to summer. Whether winter or summer, storms prevented us from moving, but not much beyond a day or two. Building an ice road was a costly process, and we often complained that we wished we could charge a toll for the number of people who used it for fishing access.

Heavy snow that year meant Paul was plowing every few days. The banks got higher and higher. Strong northwesterly winds blew snow in all directions like dust storms, coming to rest in drifts inside the ice road berms. The road diminished in width as the winter wore on. Sometimes Paul would stop to see us. Sometimes not. We had become good friends. With the use of the ice road, we were able to visit him and his girlfriend at their home. He was a gracious host, cooking us battered whitefish and serving food aplenty. All too frequently, there was too much drinking, but still we valued our time together. Jim would sense the exact right moment to leave before Paul would become vexed about something or someone.

Paul arrived after dark one night just after supper. His familiar "Yoah" could be heard from inside the cabin, with Sekima rushing to the cabin door to greet his friend. He was in good spirits, and there was no doubt that he had been drinking heavily.

He was a big man, kindhearted, but unpredictable when drinking. He reminded me of the grade school pretty blonde boy who teased just to see if someone would react to his goading. Not a bully, just a baiter. It never lasted long between Paul and Jim. Jim was by weight and height Paul's equal, and Jim simply would not react. If he did, it was because Paul refused to relent, and then it was over quickly. Paul was not prepared for a physical confrontation with Jim. Paul would turn mellow and demonstrate his friendship with a big hug.

He only wanted a beer that night, to get him home. He told us he had been drinking with Black Jack, Royal Crown whiskey in the fish shack. They had polished off a twenty-six-ounce bottle. He was visibly drunk, some balance issues, and a definite slur. We did not have any beer. We would not have given him any if we had it. There was no point in cautioning him. He would not listen to anyone, straight or drunk. He could not stay. His wolfhound was inside at home, and the fires would be going out. His girlfriend was not there. He left.

We sat in front of our fireplace reading, coal oil lantern above us; it was less than an hour later when we heard banging on the door. It was Paul.

I listened as Jim conversed with him.

"I got the goddamned plow stuck. Black piece of shit."

"Where you at?" Jim asked.

Paul was hopping mad. He explained that he was a couple miles away. He had been plowing and hit the bank. He had one tire in the slush and wanted a shovel to dig himself out.

"Give us a few minutes, and we'll drive you back to your truck with a shovel." Paul went outside, still cursing at the truck while we got geared up for the cold.

His newest purchase, a big black Ford was easy to spot, not more than a mile from our island, in full moonlight. The moon appeared to take up most of the sky, its white reflection on the snow as bright as day. He had done a good job of getting stuck. He had obviously dropped his plow blade down for a last scrape on his way home. Plowing was a constant thing, taking care of endless drifting, and if you are driving, well, you might as well be plowing.

There had been cracking and crowning to the ice road that occurs as the snowbanks accumulate, the snow weighing down heavy. The ice road bulges in the middle and flattens away from the center. Underneath those banks, on the edges of the road, water accumulates, and because of the amount of snow, it becomes insulated and never does freeze totally. The ice is weaker there, and a dangerous place for a plow or a tire to become lodged. In extreme cold, the slush affixes to the plow or tire, freezing instantly.

The plow had dug too far into the bank. It had sucked him in, the right side of his plow and a front tire nestled in the heavy slush. It was not cold enough this night to cause too much freezing, but part of the plow and his one front tire was buried in the bank. He believed if he could just get it shoveled out a bit, he could release himself from its hold.

The V-shaped spade bounced off the hard-packed banks with little effect save for the metal ringing of colliding solids. Regardless, Paul persisted with brute force and exertion as we watched his hopeless efforts. Jim offered to drive him home, but he would have none of it.

Paul was not a stamina person. He was a sudden rush of intense physical power that bored easily. Flipping the spade to the side, he jumped in the black Ford attempting to rock it back and forth, shifting hard, forward, reverse, forward, reverse. Heavy foot on the gas pedal, whining tires becoming heated, polishing ice beneath them to a slick sheen, a slippery slick hold on the truck.

Furious now, he grabbed the spade again and applied another whopping jab into the bank that did nothing but unsteady his foothold. Enraged, he hurled the spade shovel over his head to smash furious energy denting the hood of the black Ford. It rang viciously through the silence of the night, echoing back its intensity through the granite ravines. The metal spade separated from the wooden handle. It flew upwards like a skeet disk between Jim and me, narrowly missing our heads.

Jim had had enough of the amplified display of drunken frustration. Left with a wooden handle in his hand, Paul made a last fierce thrust of brute force. He held the truck door in one hand, and with all that he had left in him, he raised his leg and kicked straight at the steering wheel of the truck. The plastic steering wheel fractured and broke.

Jim was on him now, his voice booming to get Paul's attention. "Paul, stop this right now!" he commanded. "You almost hit Connie with that spade."

Paul turned. Jim challenged him, stern and intense, standing toe to toe. "You're finished with this for tonight." Jim's tone softened, giving Paul the opportunity to back down.

Paul's anger evaporated. He no longer had the energy or the adrenaline to continue, and he simply was not up to a fight with his friend.

We drove him home that night, and the silence of his embarrassment was as quiet and revealing as the full moon. It illuminated all that we were, as friends often do, bringing light to our depths, casting shadows on what we are becoming.

That night does not tell the whole story of how the end came to be between Jim and Paul's friendship. The end was not abrupt. It was a quiet letting go, bittersweet, like the first bite of a wild plum. It is like they both knew how powerful the other was, and they cared not to experience that moment of confrontation. One day they would walk away from each other with bitterness and regret.

CHAPTER 45

ANOTHER PACK

It was cold, so cold. Snow crunched underfoot; it was like walking through a field of Weetabix. Inhaling was painful. Sekima, however, seemed to be loving every moment of it as he ran past me on the narrow path. I had to catch myself from falling into the snowbank as I avoided 110 pounds of muscled momentum.

It was nearing sunset, late January, the last I would see of this bitter, cold day. It was my typical farewell, walking the length of the island to the southwest shore, awaiting the moment when the sun became a huge fireball dropping from the sky. Even the darkest of clouds were penetrated, rimmed in orange as the sun raced to meet the horizon. Jim would usually come with me, but today he still wore a heavy robe and sat by the cookstove. He was terribly sick and weak with flu.

I was only moments behind Sekima, but he was nowhere to be found when I got to the cabin. I went first to the dock deck on the north side, as it protruded out on a point of the shoreline and gave me the best vantage point. The big island lay directly north, a short distance. It was a favorite shoreline for Sekima to explore, the frozen lake providing glorious freedom for a malamute's spirit. I saw nothing. I scoured further to other distant islands, knowing the big dog could easily be further. And there he was in the distance. And he had company.

I anticipated his pursuit of a fox. He was strong enough, dominant, and a hunter. I had seen it before but had rarely seen him get this close to one. Foxes kept their distance in the daytime, and Sekima was always visible to them a long way on the flat expanse of frozen lake. This was different. They were on the ice at the base of the distant island. He was within twenty yards, running behind at an easy lope. I thought maybe it was another dog. My breath puffed steam into the air. Suddenly, and without warning, I saw five or six figures coming down the slopes of the island from various directions. A pack of wolves; the first had been the luring female.

Sekima apparently sensed the danger quicker than I. He took off running, and the wolves followed. He was almost at the base of our shoreline, near the boathouse before they surrounded him. He was fenced off and had taken a stance. They appeared larger than Sekima, their long, angular legs giving them superior height against his stalky frame. They gave him extensive breadth, circling him in a counter clockwise pattern, but with no gap to escape.

Jim and I both thought highly of wolves. The design of Mother Nature is sophisticated. A need for the higher chain, so that overcrowding and disease does not occur, leaving the healthy animals to flourish. Wolves in particular have been persecuted, originally by ranchers who lost cattle. But it's more than that. Wolves are feared for their intelligence, the way they form a Pack, a complex hunting machine acting as a unit. Regardless of their reputation, studies show that their primary kill is old, weak, or diseased animals. Regardless of their beauty and intelligence, they are hated. Feared by man. There was no way that they expected to encounter Sekima. They were opportunists. This was a mistake!

I screamed a banshee scream from where I stood some one hundred yards away. One wolf turned and ran towards the big island. The others did not follow. The winter sun hung low and heavy in the western sky, dying quickly now as dusk rode in.

Silver-grey wolves with flowing tails danced around my friend, snarling occasionally. I took off running hard. I chose the path I had come from rather than break trail on the deep drifted snow of the shoreline. I screamed as I ran. I screamed my fear and outrage. I wailed in agony and fury. I ran. I ran down the steps to the boathouse and out onto the lake towards the Pack. They parted. They ran. Huge strides, front feet barely touching the ground, silver streaks following the blue bands between dusk and darkness, leaving me standing there screaming. Sekima raced behind them in pursuit.

Color drained from the sky. My heart pumped in my ears. I ran back up the steps to the cabin. My mind raced. If I did not reach Sekima now, he would not last the night. He thought they were playmates, perhaps, or that our Pack was running them off. There was no doubt that they were driven by food. Their caution in killing him would be based on a strong instinct for survival. He was a healthy male and they would not afford an injury. They would wear him down first.

"Wolves surrounded Sekima. He's followed them." I spoke hurriedly to Jim, rushing towards the closet. "Get the 30/30 and cartridges. I have to get better boots and a coat." I needed taller boots to get me through the drifts, a balaclava for my face, my worn Inuit coat from Cambridge Bay. I needed everything now, before there was no light left in the sky. I grabbed the big flashlight.

Jim stood swaying. He was gripped with fever. "Where did he go?"

"The big island." I loaded five cartridges into the magazine and threw the rest of the box into the big pockets of my parka.

"It's dark. You can't go looking for him now."

"It's not dark out yet." I glanced at the window. It looked dark, but I knew there was still a final phase before images would disappear completely. It was unrecognizable from the inside. All the more reason to run again. I threw the gun harness over my shoulder.

The drifting snow slowed my progress. I could not run in it. My pace was quick. It was cold, so cold, and I felt none of it. I dared not use the flashlight. I would lose any ability to see the landscape ahead of me as the light stole images from my retinas.

"Sekima!" The crunching of the snow was deafening. I stopped. I shouted his name. "Sekima!" I called wildly, and I heard him call back. A howl, a familiar voice, a certainty of the blood still running through him. *Please God let him be safe.*

I could hear Jim behind me. His voice boomed. "Sekima."

His voice traveled so much further than mine. I knew how terrible he must feel. He could barely rise that morning. I knew it was all about the three of us. It was our Pack. We were a unit. We hunted together. We played together. We guarded together. We protected each other.

I saw Sekima, in the last of the fading light, jumping off the big island to the snow-covered lake. There he was, as delighted and joyous as when he'd left. Proud, majestic head in the air, tail broad and tightly curled, loping with ease and confidence, wondering what all the fuss was about. Wondering why we had not been with him in pursuit. He raced towards home ahead of me, to the spot where they had circled him. He took the pleasure of stopping to mark his territory. He was king.

CHAPTER 46

FRAGMENTED

"The brochures are very late this year. Everyone knows that it is going to just kill us if they don't get mailed in the next two weeks." Donald let his head droop.

We sat in the front office, a couch typically used for guest arrivals, chairs gathered loosely around for a meeting. Donald had insisted that his three children be present.

I had heard this same plea, with its distinctive ring of "poor me," on many occasions already. It was just one more characteristic that I disliked. It was unbecoming of a man who had any pride. Usually, he demonstrated an overabundance of arrogance. Resorting to pity was pathetic. It was just another means of manipulating others. Carlie sat off to his side, worried look on her face, occasionally glancing down at her clasped hands as though searching for answers. I had not only heard this same kind of plea from Donald before, but I also recognized that it had something to do with Carlie not completing a task she was responsible for.

"Don, we'll do whatever it takes. Brenda and I will be here over Christmas, and even if we have to work Christmas, we'll do it, big guy." Mike was an ambitious young salesman who had missed having a father in his formative years. He needed so badly to belong and be recognized. Donald fed him with just enough tasty assurances of things to come. Mike would bend over backwards to please him, hoping for rewards along the way. Here was yet another life in which Donald recognized weakness.

Donald's twenty-three-year-old son, Donald Jr., along with his girlfriend, Gwen, had come in for the meeting. They ran the daily operations of an outpost camp, and in the winter Donald's son joined him at tradeshows. His daughter, Allison, was the hostess of a small resort nearby. Both children believed their participation in the family business during the summer months was more than enough contribution. And perhaps it was because their father demanded they be there from morning to night. They were his eyes and ears. They reluctantly joined the sporadic fall and winter meetings at their father's request, ultimately fearing their presence may initiate a work effort. They were not going to work any longer. They felt no need to listen to their father any longer.

Allison, the daughter, and Gwen, the girlfriend, demonstrated their disapproval by wearing gaily-colored sleepwear to the nine a.m. meeting. Gwen toted an extra twenty-five pounds, but, with a petite face and large breasts, her weight could be veiled. She wore a sporty fitted bra under a turquoise spandex top, which gave her lots of cleavage, and the set matched her pink-and-turquoise butterfly cotton pajama bottoms. Her blonde, straight, shoulder-length hair was brushed glossy, and her eyes were shadowed dark enough for evening wear.

Allison could not compete with Gwen. Both girls were just over the five-foot mark, but Allison did not have a waste line, and her boobs were small and insignificant. She still had firm baby fat. She chose the full sleepwear effect, covering herself completely in a bumblebee pattern, with "Bite Me" written in bright pink across her ass. She wore no makeup, but adorned herself with a new Rolex that her father had just bought her for her twentieth birthday. Allison had a cute, homespun face with adorable dimples. Had she been a shy girl, she would have appeared fresh and perhaps event innocent, but that was not Allison.

Allison showed her displeasure with Mike's comment by exiting towards the bathroom. She gained an audience as she proceeded to bang on the bathroom door.

"CJ, get your ass out of there. I have to go to the bathroom."

"I don't know if you're going to want to come in here," he hollered back.

"CJ, NOW!" Allison was close to screaming.

The door opened slightly. CJ slid his slim body through the slight opening he had made. With one hand he held onto the doorknob and with the other he fanned his face. The youngest of the Nutt family, he was just reaching puberty, acne, and attitude. He would turn out to be the most violent and dangerous of the family.

Donald seemed the only one oblivious to the commotion his daughter and son were creating. He was focused on the path he had set for the meeting and was accustomed to their noisy bantering.

"Thanks, Mike. I know you're always here for me, buddy. There's sixty thousand brochures that have to go out, and they arrive tomorrow." His exclusion of everyone else created small tremors of competitiveness and hostility.

"CJ," Allison bellowed, immediately followed by the distinctive slap of a hand on flesh.

CJ grabbed Allison's wrist tightly in his hand, his face flushed with anger. His ball cap had fallen partially over one dangerous blue eye. "Now what did you go do that for, Allie?" He pushed her backwards. Although he weighed considerably less, he was much taller than his sister and much more agile. She resisted by stabbing at him with her free arm.

Donald Jr. embarrassed by his siblings, pleaded for his father's intervention which was ignored.

"We'll do it. Everybody will pitch in and help," Mike piped up, a huge wide mouth showing glistening teeth. He nodded his head up and down, looking around the room for others to acknowledge their loyalties.

"We're going to visit my folks in Toronto on Friday." Gwen directed her comment to Mike. If looks could kill. "Look, Mike. You don't have any idea how hard Don and I work during the summer. We need a break before the sport shows start up." She reapplied her clear lip gloss, smacking her lips together, daring Mike to challenge her.

"I'm just saying that if Don thinks we have to do this, which we do, right, Don? We should step in and get the job done." Mike paused, giving Donald enough time to raise his lowered head, his shoulders slouched, elbows on his knees, and nod with the defeated look of a beaten man asking for his last meal.

"I think what Gwen is saying Mike is that my dad has known about our trip for some time now. There's not much we can do to change the dates." Having spoken, Don Jr. returned his thoughts and focus to something outside in the parking lot. He often had a distant faraway look, as though he had just smoked a reefer. He was good-looking in a way, the blonde hair, the blue eyes, and the upper body that he was working on, except for the weak chin and those same weak drooping shoulders like his dad. He was so difficult to engage. It was hard to know whether that blank look was lack of understanding or a mind that was adrift on another planet.

The disorderly way that the family interacted was typical. They saw no reason to change their behavior because of a meeting. The staff twisted uncomfortably in their chairs. I was mesmerized by the outward display of hostility and aggression, and even more amazed that Donald chose not to end it. I looked around the room, noting the resigned looks on the reservation clerks' faces. There were only a few people in the room engaged, and it was best to leave it that way.

"Mike, it's not your decision." Gwen glared.

Gwen and Mike argued back and forth. Allison still fuming

over her little brother piped in to ridicule Mike about his attempts to have authority when he clearly had none.

Gwen would not relent. "You're nothing but a brown noser, Mike," Gwen spat, "and it's not going to get you as far as you think. You are not part of this family."

Don Jr. quietly nudged his girlfriend to silence her. It had little effect. Both Gwen and Allison continued to take jabs at Mike.

I had seen enough. "Look," I said, "we need to get back on track here and handle the issue of how to get these brochures out. Carlie, how many can be done in a day?"

Although I tried to get Carlie to explain how many people for how many days it would take, she seemed unable to answer. It had never occurred to her to define the solution logistically.

Gwen had slid herself under Don Jr.'s arm with a petulant look of defiance, but she was, for the moment, quiet.

"Carlie, you just figure out how to get them out as quickly as possible," Donald said quietly. He appeared totally crushed, as though his life had fallen apart. "Just make sure it happens, okay? It's not worth all this fighting with my family."

I looked down at my blank notepad. The whole thing was starting to confuse me. Donald avoided speaking to his family. Why would he let this embarrassing situation last so long? He obviously knew that Don and Gwen were not going to be available, but he said nothing. Why? He had asked for the extra effort from his staff, and most of them were genuinely there to please him. Why were his children not at least attempting to be supportive? The meeting had a purpose, or so I'd thought, but there was no resolution. Instead, the air was filled with hostility, guilt, and chaos. As usual, there was no plan. I would learn over the years that Donald really never did have a plan. He had a business model that he repeated over and over. It worked. The lake provided free fish and an adventure that people were willing to pay well for. He thrived with high US to

Canadian exchange rates. His rates were always in US dollars to take advantage of a struggling Canadian dollar. His packages were complete—boat, guide, food, and accommodations. Even the store gift shop items were tagged in US prices. Beyond that business model, he planned only to impress. There was no plan to deal with recurring problems that were inherent with a seasonal operation. There was no fun in planning.

Getting the brochures out had been handed back to Carlie. The ordering of the brochures and their distribution was her responsibility. It had been her responsibility all along. I had seen this played out in other scenarios. Carlie lacked planning and prioritizing. Subsequently, things often fell through the cracks, there were inefficiencies and costly mistakes. This was just one of them. She had known the deadline for the designer and printing firm, but she had been working on something else. She had known this was going to happen weeks ago but had taken no measures to course correct. It was always the same. She would be distraught and panic. She would seek out Donald. She could not cope and did not know what to do. I am sure she shed tears. He would save her. Hold a meeting. Try to get everyone involved. Sometimes it worked. Sometimes it did not.

There was something vastly missing in Donald's family. I included Carlie in their family because of her relationship with Donald. I tried to relate it to my little Pack. *What was missing for them?* They were interconnected but not unified. They were dependent but not cohesive. They were fragmented with seemingly conflicting or independent paths. There were no innate attributes that led them to work together, to protect each other. Their egos perpetuated the cycle of self-fulfillment, even within their own Pack. Their natural instinct was polluted by fabricated fears and rationalizations that had nothing to do with survival, like a cloud covering the sun on a perfectly clear day. The seeds of their thoughts carried far and in every direction. They failed, to act as one.

CHAPTER 47

IN THE WILD

We had plenty of deer. Cooking wild game was one of the things we were both good at. Hot and quick is the method. It can be delicate or leathery. Largely overcooked, it can resemble a leather shoe hide, but delicately prepared, it can be like melt-in-your-mouth puffed pastry. On the other hand, a stew cooked all day on the top of our wood heater would do an excellent job of tenderizing the meat. It was the backup this day, in case we didn't catch any fish.

We embarked to the south side of the island with our ice chisel. We were very limited financially, but we had good physical strength. We had no gas ice auger, which would typically be used to make a hole for fishing. It was over twelve inches thick and it took considerable chopping. It was similar to the ice road. Start out large, and eventually you end up with a reasonable path.

We were looking for ling cod. And so, we prepared a treble hook with a piece of red meat. We sat on lawn chairs, our backs to the wind. We'd picked a warm day, temperatures around -17, and the wind light. Several hours later, we had our catch. Big wide head, snake-like vertebrae, thick black skin. It resembled an eel. Jim would skin it. The meat would have texture. Both the texture and taste gave it its nickname—poor man's lobster. We would boil it and dip it in garlic butter. The stew would do nicely for tomorrow's meal.

It was roughly four p.m., and I had delayed supper, as the ling cod would cook quickly in boiling water. Sekima was missing. The big malamute did not like to miss his dinner. In a more populated area, he would be fenced. Here, he was no one's trouble but ours.

An hour later, still no Sekima, and it was dark.

Jim's voice carried much further than mine, and so he dressed and went outside, flashlight in hand. It was well over a half hour later that he came in. I had heard him calling relentlessly the whole time.

"He's not coming. Damn dog."

"I've put the cod in the fridge for the night."

"Why would you do that?"

"I don't know. The stew is ready. We can eat it any time. We can wait for a while. See if he shows up."

He assured me that there was nothing we could do tonight. He would try calling him again in a while.

Thirty minutes later, we decided to go outside once more. We would go in opposite directions on the island and call. We had no idea where he had gone. He'd been with us fishing. It was rare that he would venture off the south side of the island. Land masses were miles away, except for one. The one I'd gotten lost on.

When I opened the door, I felt incredible relief followed instantly by shock. There he was, Sekima, waiting outside the door, his beautiful coat stained with blood, blood around his muzzle and mostly on the underside of his jaw, extending and blotching the white of his chest.

"Oh no. There's blood everywhere," I cried.

"Calm down. Get him in here so we can take a look." Jim forcibly pushed past me and grabbed the dog's collar, leading him inside.

"What do need? A wet cloth?"

"Yes. A small bucket of water too. I have to see where the blood is coming from." Jim had already sat the dog down in our front room, soft coal oil lanterns casting shadows, the flashlight spotting across Sekima's chest.

His coat was clean. He was not bleeding. Something else was. Jim found an inch long slice through his hide, but it did not penetrate beyond.

I felt so much gratitude that he was not hurt. I could not think of anything we should have or could have done. This was the wild. The strongest survived. From the top of the food chain to the bottom of the food chain. The top layer here was wolf and bear—except for our Pack. Sekima had survived, but who had lost the battle?

We lived remote. We lived in the wild. To many, nature would appear unpredictable, but not so. There were cycles of weather. Seasons to be recognized and reckoned with. Everything appeared random, a boulder sitting on flat granite that seemed dropped from the sky, a white pine that soared above all other trees, an eagle's nest that defied ferocious westerly winds, a spotted fawn that swims across the bay with no mother, a loon with no mature flight feathers defying an eagle. There was an ebb and flow of life and death. When you live in nature, the only thing you can do is to understand your vulnerabilities, understand that anything that you build, nature can destroy.

Sekima remained anxious during the night, pacing the floor, his thick nails clicking on the old wood floors. I was relieved that each time I awoke, he was there, either wandering about in the living room, or yelping in his dreams. Whatever was out there may be hurt and suffering. I shoved the thought away to find sleep.

The morning was crisp and cold and there were plenty of chores that day, some of them daily, some of them weekly, all dependent on weather conditions. It had snowed overnight and there were paths to shovel. Sekima was his usual self, hearing mice below the snow, small creatures crawling in the grass in a natural, built-in igloo. He would cock his head side to side, leap into the air, crash with his front paws through the layers of snow. If he happened to get lucky, he would hold still until his feet felt no movement, indicating the small creature had expired. If he was unsuccessful, he would repeat the process and dive his head and massive shoulders into the snow. It was a funny sight, with just a part of his back and tail exposed above the snow cover.

We were down on our favorite deck, which we kept shoveled so we could enjoy those exquisite winter sunsets and the occasional northern borealis that danced across the sky. Not that the northern light spectacle was a rare occasion, but it was rare that we would be up much past dark.

The Pack—Jim, Sekima, and myself—saw them all at the same time. A small group of ravens, low in the sky, circling, peering down on a corner of Channel Island. Sekima was off before we had time to call him back. But Jim knew. They'd seen a carcass they could feed on. It was most likely Sekima's kill.

I waited patiently for Jim to return. I wondered how he would bury or get rid of whatever it was, as Sekima would protect his kill until there was no carcass remaining. In the winter, that could be a very long time. I laughed at the sight when I saw them coming. Jim had a rope with him and he was dragging something obviously too heavy or awkward for him to carry. Sekima flanked him, veering from left to right, grabbing the rump of the carcass as if to bite off a morsel. They left a snaky swath of indented snow behind them.

It arrived. Jim brought it up to the island. It was Sekima's kill. A fully grown adult beaver, weighing no less than fifty pounds. His mouth was wide, full, large, yellow incisors that had no doubt ripped through Sekima's fur and nicked his hide. It was a formidable foe. Jim had found him on the edge of his dam, lying on his back.

I had mixed feelings. Most of the island people hated beavers.

They built their dens, large homes of sticks and mud, below their docks, the debris floating around for the whole summer. Sometimes they built them between docks, and when the island people arrived, there was nowhere to park their boats. Their dens were almost impossible to penetrate or remove. They were like mortar. They were temporary homes, until they moved on to a better place for them to forage. They reminded me of some birds that I wanted to tell a thing or two about using the same nest. Apparently securing a mate meant that you needed to build them a new home on a yearly basis.

In some instances, they built dams on small creeks that would break when spring rains came, pond water tumbling down with a wake of destruction. Or they simply came to your island and took what they could find, poplar, birch, and even small oak. Their teeth required constant use to curb the continuing growth.

The smell of their drying pelts in my parents' basement had not been an unpleasant odor. It was not a pungent scent. It smelled vaguely of a mix of dried leaves basting in olive oil. The dried hides were merely supplemental income for my family, and a way for my dad to control their population.

Jim lay the beaver near the back door. Sekima was immediately on it. Its body was frozen, the hide thick and glossy with its winter coat. There was dried blood around the puncture wounds on the thick neck. They would not have been enough to kill the animal; Sekima had no doubt broken its neck with a powerful snap. For the rest of the day, Sekima lay in the snow, occasionally gnawing at it, but mostly protecting his kill. If we passed too close while doing our chores, he would growl, curling his lips, showing his short incisors and long canine teeth. We let the day pass, respecting that it was his.

By nightfall, he had not moved. It was time. I was not the alpha in this pack. I watched. Sekima gave all the resistance he could muster, but in the end Jim dominated. Sekima was rewarded inside with a bowl of food covered with fish stock. Jim slipped out, hauling the frozen carcass to the boathouse.

It had to be removed. It was evident that Sekima would worry over it until there were no remains, and that would take a very long time. There was no easy way to get rid of it that Sekima would not track. The boat house roof was the only option. Jim was forced to tow it up a ladder and push it as far as he could on the rolled asphalt surface. In the morning, Sekima retraced Jim's trail but as hard as he tried to locate the beaver, it was nowhere to be found. By spring, we would have to return its carcass to the wild on some other island, but for now it would remain hidden.

CHAPTER 48

DOG TROUBLE

It was several months later and I was back at work. Our isolation had faded away. It remained calm at the resort. Office staff were busily taking reservations. Gina had been replaced. A new Reservations Manager was at the helm. I was busy inputting data for new employees and focusing on policy and procedures that were inadequate or nonexistent.

The sport shows continued, and it seemed that they were enough to keep Donald busy and tired, even when he would return for a week or two at a time. His eldest son joined him at several shows. Allison made infrequent visits to the office for fanfare, or when she was lonely.

Christopher, nicknamed CJ by his family had just turned into a teenager. Carlie pretended to control him, pretended to be motherly, and pretended to discipline him when necessary. She gave him lectures about things he wore, combing his bed head, or vulgar language. Carlie was also responsible for looking after Larky, their purebred golden retriever. The dog would come into the office each day when CJ went to school. Donald had encouraged and guilted her into taking on additional responsibilities. This was all part of the family culture.

CJ clearly had similar characteristics to his father. A staff member would drive him to the bus pick-up spot. Sometimes he went. Sometimes he did not. Sometimes he behaved. Most times he did not. He was insulting, disrespectful, and extremely angry. He cared for no one.

Larky had been lethargic. For a young dog, he was listless; he barely moved from his dog bed in the office. Carlie instructed one of the maintenance crew, Jerome, to take the dog to the veterinarian after dropping off CJ for school. The report from the vet's office was very disturbing. They had found a sprayed pattern from BB gun pellets across the dog's rump and back legs, penetrating through his hide and into the soft tissue. Some infection was already occurring. The question was who had done it, and why would someone do something so cruel to an animal? Larky did not look like a wolf, like Sekima, nor was he much of an outdoor dog. The shots appeared not to have been fired with the intention to kill, but without treatment the wounds were deadly.

CJ arrived as usual from school about four p.m., and Carlie was quick to question him. "CJ, Larky is on medication because his ass was full of BBs. I don't suppose you know anything about that?" She cocked her head slightly and pursed her lips. Carlie was street smart. She did not have beyond a Grade 12 education, but she had been disciplined as a Cadet, and she came with a lot of natural instinct for people. She was definitely well-versed in being lied to. Donald had provided her with all of that experience.

CJ looked away, as though he could avoid the persecution. He was still too young to make things up quickly. His pimpled face had flushed. There were obvious signs that he was guilty.

"Well, CJ, why did you shoot Larky with your BB gun?" Carlie had time enough during the day to build up sufficient anger. She knew that CJ was the only possible person responsible. She stood up from her desk as CJ made way for his exit out the door.

"Look here, mister. You're not going home until you answer my question." Standing only inches above his height, she blocked the doorway.

"And what are you going to do about it if I did?" he boldly snapped.

"If you were my kid, I'd be strapping your ass so it hurt like Larky's." As I listened from the copy machine, I could not help but think that she had some guts. She was treating him like the angry little kid that he was. No discipline, no responsibilities, no guidance.

"You're not my mother. Call my dad. Do whatever you want. I'm taking Larky with me." He looked back at the dog who was resting on his dog bed, looking up at both of them with those sad, hurting dog eyes.

"Come on, Larky. Come on." The dog struggled to his feet, probably a bit confused from the medication. CJ was still his master.

There was nothing Carlie could do. "I'll be taking this up with your dad."

"Go right ahead, *Carleee*." He accentuated her name as though it was a piece of dirt in his mouth.

And that was the end of it then. Of course, Carlie told Donald. Of course, the response was to make sure that Larky was taken care of by the vet, and that Carlie administered the medication. Of course, Donald said he would talk to CJ.

CJ wasn't Donald's pride and joy. His eldest son was his pride and joy. He was Donald Jr. III. His daughter was fondly referred to as Princess Allison. And then there was CJ, the youngest, born into the most bitter time of his parents' marriage. Their mother had not been responsible or there for the youngest child, as she preferred truckers and their bunks. Donald had the money, and I guess he'd thought that would be enough. Money was a short-term fix, but eventually it was not. It would get much worse.

Some children have a desire to see what happens when you step on a toad. Some to throw a cat by its tail. Some to whip their pony. Sometimes, a kid hurts so much inside after doing something like that, they do not ever want to do it again. Some relish and thrive on cruelty, from youth to old age. Some parents are able to correct the behavior, recognizing that this is a paramount time for development of a child's psyche. Some parents, like Donald, did not really see a need, or didn't notice.

At the time I had more empathy towards the dog than I did for what Christopher may have been experiencing. Larky was a beautiful golden retriever. I had watched during the summer as Donald took him on his daily shore lunch boat rides, saying, "Come, Larky. Let's go buddy." He seemed to truly love the dog.

It was so difficult to understand, but at the same time, it wasn't. Larky was a commodity to Donald. He was a symbol of a wholesome family, and to some extent there was prestige in a pedigree. It was the reason the dog existed. His children existed—they, too, symbolized a wholesome family. He would lavish them with gifts, with words of love and praise, in front of people. He would have seasonal initiation meetings for new staff, flaunting his children as objects of his affections. "They are my family, don't mess with them, or there will be consequences." Then he would name those who were most loyal in order. I was included for a while.

There was only one reason for the touting. Loyalty. Devotion to him.

CHAPTER 49

OUR RETURN

The winter passed and spring was early. Torrential rains took the snow away, leaving the ice polished and defenseless to the rays of sun. The ice road banks were barely recognizable aside from dotted auger holes in numerous places. Lazy fisherman or those without snow machines, fished barely off the road in their trucks. Now, the holes appeared as lunar eclipses, dark and silent. The start of the road on mainland was full of mud, thick tracks where people had gotten stuck, or broken the ice away. We had given up traveling by vehicle, and I was back to dog sledding across the expanse. It would not be long now.

It was evident that I was the last on the lake. Sekima and I took no more than twenty minutes to cross to mainland. The ice was firm in the morning, save for some gaps, no more than six inches of crossing open water. Long expanses of cracking, the effects of thawing and freezing, expanding and contracting against the shoreline. Sometimes it would cause high ridges as the ice floes pushed against each other, a battle of tremendous power. But in the spring, they relaxed, as though satisfied that it was time to fall away from each other, to make way for the new.

I was aware of the heat of the day. Sekima was patient. He waited in our truck for the day to pass, was let out several times to do his business while I hurriedly finished work, avoiding breaks and lunch. We were finally able to go. I knew this would likely be the last time over the ice. Brian was prepared to do a few trips with the windjammer until the boat was launched. It would not be long. The bays were open, and Whitefish would follow in due time.

I pushed off from the point. Full visibility and the sun still relatively high in the sky, for spring was upon us. The purple toboggan was retired. The cedar kick-sled with Teflon runners glided smoothly behind Sekima as he trotted along. He needed no help from me. I approached one of the gaps that had receded in the morning and was happy to see that the ice had shifted. It was a mere crack forming a long line from north to south.

There was a small island just east of us, where friends of ours from Minnesota lived; they came up for most of the summer. Their island sat some three hundred yards or more from a larger island. The larger island was traditionally the place where trout fisherman set their sights. Its granite face towered above, and towered below to depths of 150 feet.

I blinked several times as I reached that spot. Between the two islands was another gap, this one over six feet wide, dangerously blue, lapping small waves onto the ice. The ice was thick, that I was sure of. It had not turned black; it was at least two feet thick, but I could not cross. It lay across my path, bridging our friend's island with the big island. The wind had shifted the ice during the day. I could see our island in the distance, so close, so far away.

I could have turned back then. I could have taken lodging at the resort, or somewhere in town. I could have phoned Brian to bring me out in the morning in his windjammer. I did not want to wait. I rationalized that Jim would be frantic when I did not return. I rationalized that I needed to be home. Like an addict that needs their next fix, I needed to be home.

I knew our friends' island well. We had been there many times. It was less than a half-acre. The fissure snaked on both sides, north to south, but I still had passage to the island on the east side. I could traverse over the island and make my way off on the other side, a clear shot from there to home. As I reached the shore, I was startled as the lake boomed, a thunderous reverberation. I instinctively felt fear.

I got to the shore and removed the leads from Sekima so that he would not get entangled in the low-lying bush. Once a few bolts were removed, I could fold the sled and carry it. It took but ten minutes for me to emerge on the west side. Sekima was already there, his nose high in the air, smelling what lay ahead. My heart sank. There was more open water here than along the gaping crack. It surrounded this part of the island, open some ten feet from shore, no doubt diminished by the sun and the earth's warmth, released waters that would soon regain hold in Whitefish Bay.

I could not see well from my vantage point. I had lost time, and I could see the sun on its retreat. I should have been able to see Jim had he been on the dock deck of our island, but I knew he would not be looking for me yet.

I made my way as quickly as I could back to my starting point on the island. Sekima followed. I had yet another decision to make—retreat to the safety of mainland or find yet another path. The lake erupted again. Loud booming like shock waves, a sonic boom. The forces of ice grinding together like icebergs colliding with each other. As I retreated from the island, the thunderous rumble was like a battle of angry gods. I thought for an instant that the ice would break apart and I would enter a black hole. I let the feeling pass as she became quiet once more.

I quickly reharnessed Sekima to the sled. I could see off in the distance to the south. I did not know how far, but the gaping crack of ice appeared to come together. Off in the distance, I could see the shoreline of mainland. I would make one last attempt at reaching our island and home.

My sense of urgency made Sekima tug hard at the traces. We followed some distance away from the fractured ice as its cut became less and less wide, the water no longer able to spill over onto the ice. I had travelled a half mile or so. As far as I could see ahead, a black rivulet continued. The lake expelled its breath once more, a deafening moan. This was it. It was not going to get better, and the further south I went, the further away I got from home.

Perhaps frightened half out of my wits, I was now reluctant to jump the two feet of water that separated me from another ice mass. I was shaken from the impasse and my unsuccessful earlier attempts. My confidence seemed to seep from my pores. I had done this very thing this morning, with ease. I knew Sekima would not hesitate, but I did not want to burden him with my weight. I got off the sled and bundled the traces so they would not hamper him in any way.

"Go Sekima, go."

He did; he was on the other side, and so was the sled. He stopped and looked back at me. I suddenly felt terribly foolish and nauseous. I realized that I had abandoned the sled that would distribute my weight. I had been unnerved, and the result was irrational behavior. *Please lord, don't let me slip.* I made it to the other side, laughing and crying all at once.

I sang the rest of the way home, like I usually did, thinking that Sekima enjoyed the variety of tune. I sang when all was well. Jim was out on the dock deck. He saw us coming. Life was good.

CHAPTER 50

JAMMING

Spring thaw and freeze were fickle, one part wanting to let go, one part wanting to enjoy the comforts of being locked in. It turned cold again, which allowed me several more days to pass to mainland. The wind changed and the ice shifted, once again bridging the water that had stopped me, bringing the pieces of the puzzle firmly in place. Only the northern shorelines still held ice, so we arranged for my final trip to mainland. I would walk the four miles without Sekima, and Brian would return me by the end of the day by windjammer. I would have to take a few days off, undetermined as to when I would have boat passage. It would not be long.

Unlike our risky return when we'd left Les and Edie's retreat, I would follow the path of the ice road. It was the thickest part of the ice, and the ridges where the snowbanks had been formed were a guiding corridor.

I left early from work. I felt energized and romantic. It was such a great feeling to pick up mail and a few groceries. I made a stop at the liquor store for a bottle of white wine before hurrying down to the Municipal dock where Brian had parked. He was waiting patiently for me and accepted my apology for taking so long with a wave of his hand.

Brian took the uppermost prop blade and gave it a swift snap. The first attempt gave a bit of engine noise that rattled short of starting. He repeated the process, stepping back quickly as the blades whirred with the start of the motor. I wondered how many people had lost a limb doing that.

He fingered a small piece of wood attached to the decking of the windjammer. It was attached to a cable that would move the big fan blades from right to left allowing him to steer. Another wire was attached to a throttle which would vary his speed as it gave the machine more or less gas. There was barely any throttle required to propel the windjammer over the slippery spring ice. We were off.

The windjammer glided across the ice at incredible speed. The slightest hollow or dent in the ice tossed me from the wooden seat. I grasped the low wooden edge of the boat and held on for the ride.

I glanced sideways at Brian. The black toque he wore low on his brow was barely a contrast to his dark skin and deep brown eyes. There was a serious calm in those eyes that spoke magnitudes. They spoke of intelligence and wisdom. They spoke of pleasure. The kind of pleasure that comes with understanding and embracing all that nature has to offer.

I took a deep breath of fresh, spring air. The forest of evergreens that blanketed the islands stood as a solid mass on the shorelines, framed by significant white pine giants that rose like high rise buildings against a pool of pale blue sky. Spring snow had shrunk and molded to the contours of the land like a latex glove.

The little boat hurtled forward. I anticipated each bounce. The blemishes on the ice jolted the windjammer and tried to shake me loose. Each significant ripple that I saw in the ice, I met by lifting myself slightly off the seat. It helped ease the stress to my back and my emotions.

The wind was hungry as it swept across the open lake, blowing us slightly sideways as Brian fought to course correct. Conditions never seemed to stay constant for long on the lake. Brian tucked the windjammer behind an island and followed the shoreline north. I recognized he was taking a back way that would lead to our island. It would take us out of our way, but it would keep us out of the crosswinds that Brian struggled with. It was a pretty route that rapidly narrowed between the islands with the curling direction of a winding river. As we approached its midpoint, the decaying ice gave way to water. The shallow water with its rock bottom had already melted. This was called Canoe Channel for a reason.

The engine was at full throttle through the breaking ice and into the water. Brian's boat was floatable. Barely. He had built it himself, and it was primarily meant to pass through short sections of open water quickly. Its purpose was to take its passengers from ice to water and out again safely and quickly. Or water to ice, and out again, safely.

The sapphire water cradled us as we entered it. I felt the true emergence of spring as we meandered through the channel. This was it. The lake was breaking loose, opening and widening, and it would waste away the winter as gradually and surely as the sun rising and setting. Our island, not more than two miles away, was still very well encased in ice.

Brian gave one more thrust to the engine to climb onto the thick floating ice at the end of the channel. It looked like thick ice floes beyond for at least a mile. With engine revved, we barely made it up on the ice, and then we limped forward, covering a few feet before grinding to a halt. Brian released the cable to the gas line, recognizing a serious problem.

He hopped out on the floating ice with the agility of someone in their twenties, and quickly grabbed a short rope connected to the front of the boat. With one leap he was on the shoreline of a small island that was a few feet away. The direction we had come from was open water amidst groups of small islands. In front of us, large chunks of ice floated like icebergs, until they appeared as a solid mass beyond.

I watched with curiosity as this little man probed the underside of the boat with his makeshift paddle. I jumped the short distance to the shoreline, realizing that my weight would not help him investigate the hull of the boat. I remained silent, not wanting to interrupt his train of thought, even though I was anxious to know our plight.

"Well, I'll be darned." He finally spoke. "One of the glides has come loose and is lodged sideways."

"What do you mean, glides?" I asked.

"The two Teflon strips that run front to back of the boat. That's what the boat slides on," he explained. "Wood wouldn't slide on the ice." He pried the boat up on its side a few inches for me to see what he meant.

I bent down and looked underneath. Sure enough, there was a strip of very thick plastic, about three inches wide, dangling loosely from the bottom of the boat. It was no longer front to back as he had explained. It was at an angle to the sides of the boat and would obviously prevent the boat from moving forward. It must have come loose in the water.

"So now what?" I asked.

"Well, I've got to find something, some way of fixing it." Brian jumped back into the boat and started rummaging. "I only have a few wrenches to fix the motor."

I glanced at my watch. It was close to four p.m. We had another hour or so of daylight.

"What can I do?" I asked.

He explained that he needed flat rocks to act like a jack under the boat. He would need them to raise the boat up at least eight inches so that he could work under it.

I noticed he had given up on his tool kit and was now searching the floor of the boat. "Okay. I'll get some rocks."

Rocks were not hard to find. Not here on the Canadian Shield.

There were plenty the size of a large frying pan that would do nicely. I took note of some that would be good but were too heavy for me to lift.

"There's some good luck." Brian raised his gloved hand to show me the three two-inch nails he had found. Two of them were slightly bent. "We were hauling some decking to fix someone's boathouse, and these nails must have fallen out of our bucket."

"So, you use nails to attach the glides to your boat. Doesn't that cause holes for the water to come in?" I laughed. I felt relief at his find and threw a flattened rock close to the boat.

"I'd normally use a screw that wouldn't go all the way through, but I'm just lucky to have found these nails. I've never had this happen before."

I suddenly felt badly. I realized that if it was not for me wanting a ride back, this would not have happened. He would not have placed himself on the lake when it was this windy. He would not have come down Canoe Channel through the water. He probably would not have had his ski fall off, nor put holes in his boat.

"Oh, Brian. I feel responsible. You wouldn't be out here tonight if it wasn't for me."

"This could have happened any time and likely would have. As far as putting holes in the boat, have you not noticed how many places the water comes in?" He grinned.

"Noooo."

"I just didn't want to frighten you any. The faster we go, the less water can stay in the boat." He jumped to the shore, laughing.

"So that's why you drive so fast!" I took up his humor. "Over here. There's a nice big flat rock that was too heavy for me."

Brian wiggled the rock free. Even for him, it would be quite heavy. He picked up one corner and rolled it on its back. A large garter snake lay motionlessly where the rock had rested.

I jumped back, barely containing a scream. "I don't like snakes!"

"Oh, this guy isn't going to hurt you. He's asleep for a while yet." Brian rolled the rock several more times towards the boat.

I knew they did not bite, but I did not like them anyways. I distanced myself from the snake.

"Most people feel that way. They've never bothered me."

It took us several minutes to stack the rocks up in two piles. Brian lifted the side of the boat so that I could place another rock on top of the last. We then added to the first pile. And so, back and forth we went, until we had almost ten inches of distance from the bottom of one side of the boat to the ground. The glide dangled loosely, held only in one spot by a screw.

Using a small rock, we straightened the bent nails. "I can use this little rock as a hammer. I'm not sure how easy it's going to be to get this nail through that Teflon." Brian was already on his back squirming his way under the boat.

"You must be a lucky girl," he announced. "These nails are just a little bit bigger than the holes already there. They should hold for the rest of the trip."

"I'm not sure about the lucky part," I said. "How long do you think it would have taken for your family to start looking for you if you didn't show up before dark?"

"They wouldn't be looking for me for at least a couple of days." I was in disbelief.

"They'd just think I went ahead to my trapper's shack. It's happened before."

"What's happened before? You going to the trapper's shack, or you breaking down and having to stay out in the bush overnight?"

"Both." He shimmied from under the boat. "That should do it."

Twenty minutes later, the outline of the island appeared through the shadows of nightfall. I quickly thanked the heavens. Jim met us at the shoreline and helped me unload my few parcels. Brian was away quickly and wordlessly, with a wave to us both. The roar of the engine could be heard long beyond our ability to see the boat through the envelope of darkness.

Brian and I rarely spoke much, but we had a connection that ran deep. Perhaps it was our heritage, perhaps it was our affinity for nature. It was usually just the windjammer engine roaring in our ears, or running into each other at the grocery store in town. We exchanged smiles that meant more than words could ever say.

CHAPTER 51

CARLIE

That summer seemed easy enough. Not for Carlie, though. She had a boyfriend. Maybe that is why Donald became so unhinged with her. Maybe it was simply that Carlie was exposed to employees that made her think differently of Donald. They were shedding light on him, a light she had not seen before. We had hired older management people. I volunteered to do the interviewing of senior staff, and gave Donald an end list. He liked the idea. He got several choices and the final say. They proved to be all good people, smart people, and effective. They were smarter than Donald. Enough to realize who Donald was, how to stroke his ego, and how to get the job done. It came with a price to Carlie.

Donald was relentless with her. *The guides are stealing from me. A cooler disappeared with all the pop last week. Do something. The grounds keepers are driving the four-wheelers after hours. Stop them. Guest services forgot to bring snacks to the cabin. Get someone that can. My boat wasn't gassed last night. Fix it, so it never happens again. We have a big check out on Sunday. I know it's your day off, but you will need to work.*

Carlie lost hair. Her lips broke into cold sores. Ugly sores of stress.

Jim was still accustomed to meeting me at the boathouse when the wind was coming from the south, hitting the boat broadside. It was difficult in those conditions. Today I could not get it right. As I neared the boathouse entrance, I veered too far left and overshot the opening. I made several more attempts.

Jim was getting frustrated with me. "You're coming in too slow. You have to come in under power."

I circled again and repeated the same thing. He was waving at me trying to get my attention. I just would not listen. I finally came in almost diagonal to the opening, cut the motor and threw him the stern rope. He pulled me back parallel to the platform.

"What were you doing? You've done this before."

"You wouldn't do any better under these conditions," I snapped.

"That may be true, but you've done it many times."

He had supper ready for me. I was not hungry. I had lost my appetite. Although I appeared to be the calm person amidst most crises at the resort, I was losing my composure. The anger had dissipated, and I felt battered and weary.

"What did he do this time?" Jim finished the last bite of his fish and shoved his plate off to the side.

I explained to him what had happened during the day, like most days. More battering. More manipulation. It was not unusual for me to come home with a troubled mind. A week could not pass without something drastic happening.

"It sounds like Carlie set herself up again, so why are you so upset?" He took both our plates from the table and set them on the counter. He returned, waiting for my response.

"I don't know. It's not over. It never is. I know Carlie had lots of opportunity to avoid any crisis, but I feel bad for her."

I tried to explain it to him. Carlie had come into my office, visibly shaken, dabbing frantically at her eyes to remove teared mascara. I tried talking to her, but all she said was some day he would be the death of her. She did not have time to talk. She had people checking out. I knew he was holding her responsible for any slight misstep. I could only imagine what pressure she was under. He had her running in every direction.

"Look, it's not your problem. She's been doing this for a very long time. She got herself into the situation, and she's the only one that can get herself out. You do what you need to do. Nothing more."

I know he always had sound advice but I could not help feeling badly. I had seen the bald spot on the back of Carlie's head where hair was falling out. I saw massive cold sores come overnight. She was younger than me by at least ten years and so stressed. Part of that stress was because she was owning some truths that she had never seen before. Over the months, Carlie had finally started confiding in me and others. We tried to help her see Donald for who he really was. I tried to get her to see the good part of her, the healthy part of her. Fragments of the spider web were breaking. But how would she repair? I knew it was a slow process. Slow and steady. I finally had her trust.

Regardless of Jim's advice, I could wait no longer. I felt the stirring, that undeniable instinct that the waiting was over. I had observed. I had been patient. I ducked down low so as to not be seen, like the vole beneath the ground avoiding the sunlight, avoiding the hawk above. But that does not mean that their population doesn't sustain or grow. Like drops of water on a pond that spread ripples over the surface, Carlie was feeling different vibrations. Those tremors would grow, increasing in speed and intensity. Given time and a bit of coaxing, the mirror would crack and shatter.

CHAPTER 52

EARTH, AIR, FIRE & WATER

I had a fondness for the old Celtic rituals I had read about. Their appreciation of nature and its rhythms were parallel to my own gratitude. I believed we needed strength from something beyond ourselves, something more tangible than my prayers, and so I looked towards nature. Nature had brought the Pack together; nature was our glue.

We planned the weekend to go to a special spot on an island that rose high out of the lake. We would do something symbolic to demonstrate the power of our unity. We needed to find the four elements of nature, the four basic energies of the universe—earth, air, fire and water. On finding these things, we would say a small prayer.

We had not been out exploring together for some time. Summer was the busiest time. Our steps were light. Our hearts joyful. Sekima bounded up the island, seeking his own treasures. We were delighted to quickly find our first symbol. It was a smooth grey poplar, with a beaver-made stub that had been etched by fire on one side. It was old. Jim placed it in our backpack, and we were off. We climbed the steep wall to the top of the island, broken, rigid granite providing stepping stones, arms of crooked pine assisting with our ascent.

Recent rain provided us with what we were looking for next. A small pool of water cupped in a bowl of stone. I had brought a little glass vessel for just this purpose. We could have taken water from the lake, but that just seemed too easy.

Our earth choice was a decaying piece of peat moss from the basin of the sphagnum bog. It was the bog we'd found when we first came to the island. Central to the large two-hundred-acre island, the granite would have been carved out by receding glaciers, leaving a bowl for water to accumulate. Lanky black spruce with bulbous tops penetrated the perimeter. A thick carpet of sphagnum moss surrounded the acidic murky pool. The moss moved underfoot, the heavy mass floating and thick. We always tread the same path, careful to avoid the delicate carnivorous pitcher plan and respectful of the fragile ecosystem.

We had agreed upon a feather for air. Air was a representation of lightness and energy, "excitement in the air." Its values were the new and untried. Appropriate for our goal of finding new ways to deal with obstacles that might come in our path.

Our search for a feather was intensive. The ground cover was a maze of mosses, juniper, broken branches, and rocks, thrown randomly in nature's orderly fashion. We learned quickly that the habitat was not suitable for birds. It was largely made up of spruce and jack pine, with very little attraction of seed or berry producing shrubs and grasses. We split up to search further, arranging to meet back at our chosen observation point. We both came back emptyhanded, each hoping that the other had found what we needed. As we strode towards each other, we could not help but hurry our stride to beat each other to the punch. There it lay. A single flight feather from an eagle. It was the sign we needed.

We recited our small prayer, gratitude for the powers of Mother Nature, and a request to be blessed by these powers in our life. We sat silently on the top of the ridge, absorbed by the highpoint advantage we had, overlooking the lake, gifted by Mother Nature in our finds.

Sekima stretched out, poised and alert on the pink granite. We felt the energies of the earth beneath us, the breath on the wind, the purity of the gleaming water, and the fire in our passion for each other. We were one. And the Pack was together.

CHAPTER 53

THE END

It was fall again. Seasons changed, as did our lives. Jim was ever-expanding his horizons. He had taken on construction projects with Paul. He had salvaged interior doors, windows, and finishing pine whenever he heard of someone doing a renovation. One man's throwaway was another's riches. We were able to save enough money to pay Paul to excavate a foundation for a bedroom and future bath. At the same time, we put in a permanent waterline to a submersible pump in the lake. The addition had a partial cellar below it with a five-hundred-gallon holding tank for water. We purchased a generator that would handle the load. After the foundation and cellar were in place, we worked night and day ourselves building the addition. Just like we had when we'd begun, we worked side by side, one board at a time. We could not afford to build a septic, and so we waited. For now, the bathroom lay idle.

Out of acquaintances we built friendships, but it was always just the three of us. The Pack became stronger. We were successful in our hunts. We were not making the same mistakes. We were heeding nature's teachings as best we could. We were becoming more independent.

It was that independence that led to the ending.

It was likely that Paul felt it the most. He had been our counsel, making recommendations and warning us of pitfalls. It compared to a parent trying to teach their children of the risks and dangers of life. He reminded me of a senior who desperately wants to validate their life by passing on their wisdom. Is there a time to recognize that sometimes you are the teacher, and sometimes you are the student?

It was a cold day. We were ready to take the boat in soon. The clouds hung heavily in the sky. A fine mist of rain had begun, turning to sleet. Loons and terns had left. Squirrels came out infrequently when the sun brought warmth to their nests. Hibernation of small animals had begun. The lake was empty, and shallow bays had begun to freeze. As usual, Paul, like ourselves looked for the final signs that would indicate the lake would transform to its sleepy state of healing.

I had seen the Promiscuous Queen dock, and I waited inside. I heard a muffled conversation and opened a window. I knew Jim was going to tell Paul that we had purchased a three-quarter-ton truck with a plow to do our own plowing this winter. We anticipated that Paul would object, would say it was a bad idea, that Jim had no experience. For us, the truck cost would cost no more than the expense of Paul plowing, and Jim did not think it would be difficult. Paul had already given us an approximation of the cost, and he had no other work out this way.

"Man, I don't understand," Paul said.

"It's something we can do ourselves. I need the truck anyways to haul wood this winter." "I don't get it."

"What, Paul, what do you not get?" Jim clearly did not want to offend Paul. He had already recognized that Paul may feel we were rejecting him in some way. We had already discussed the economics of our decisions, but also how Paul might feel.

"You know what I don't get. Plain and simple man. You are not putting your woman first. You should be building a septic field with the money so she can shit inside, instead of buying a truck for yourself."

"That's not the way it is." Jim's voice rose a notch.

"Damn right it is. We've been friends now for a while. But you are not treating her right. An outhouse, while you get a truck!"

This was going sideways. Paul was not right. We could not afford a septic field. It was ten times the cost of the truck. There was no comparison, and I was not a fragile, wanting woman.

Jim had enough. He rarely allowed himself to be overcome by anger. But at that moment, as the dark clouds swirled overhead, the rain turning to pelting sleet, he would not accept Paul's accusations. He had listened patiently to accusations, any criticism that Paul had delivered to him in the past. The line had been crossed. Never would he fail to defend me. Never would he not protect the Pack. Not now, not ever.

"I'm not talking to you anymore about this. You get the hell off this island."

They must have walked away from each other, refusing to physically fight.

I came to the door as it opened, expecting Jim. It was Paul. He spoke no words. His blonde hair was wispy and thinning. His skin was white around his eyes from wearing sunglasses most of the time. He looked sad. He reached over and took my head in his hands and gently placed a kiss on my lips. I never told Jim. It was a simple goodbye. It was the end.

CHAPTER 54

TIME TO REST

Each branch appeared to have been dipped in snow, the underside carrying more blanket than the top. Shades of green and brown penciled through, like an artist's brush, an afterthought. As the sun broke through at midday, every branch, every stem, every needle glistened in glorious splendor. Great plumes of mist billowed upwards from the lake like cloudbursts. The lake would rest soon.

Life was a slow-moving river, and we were now going downstream. Gone was the turbulent and the unexpected. Gone was the fear of my existence. There were days of tender love, joyful sharing, serene togetherness. We walked the path sometimes following, at other times, hand in hand. There had been survival moments. Survival was never a game for us. The journey we shared this far left deep roads of devotion, profound healing and untold adventure.

Winter was a mirage that let us contemplate. In nature, things go silent. So did our minds. The silence was not deafening. It transferred us to creativity, to mindfulness, to rest. It transferred the waters to healing, the trees to deep sleep, the wolves and deer to instinct.

It was winter again. All things were peaceful. Days would pass slowly until I would have to return to work. At one time, I had felt freeze-up took forever; now it seemed too short.

CHAPTER 55

ENOUGH IS ENOUGH

I had seen it coming. I'm not sure Carlie did. There was a shift in authority, a shift in positions. Donald was slowly but surely reducing her from her authority and from his personal life. Don Jr. was being groomed for Senior, to relinquish some of Donald's responsibilities. Donald had decided to hire a full-time Reservations Manager, giving Carlie less work but also less power in the direction and day-to-day activities in the office, particularly in the winter months.

Jill immediately became friends with Carlie. She was taller than Carlie, with a robust body, unblemished facial skin, high cheek bones, good proportion to her facial characteristics, and long dark hair that flowed straight and sexy down her back.

I had little time to converse with them but overheard many of the conversations, particularly about Donald. Carlie told too much, shared too much, and no doubt showed Jill a clear path to winning Donald over. Jill herself had divorced an abusive husband. Donald likely looked like an easy target, financially big gains for her, and far less offensive than her last partner.

My relationship with Carlie had changed. I wanted the best for her. I wanted her to experience who she really was. She was blunt and funny and cared so much for others. I stopped blaming her for her messed-up world.

Jill, however, I did not trust. There was no connection between us. She was friendly enough, but there was a brick wall between us. Perhaps it was because I saw the play before it happened. Perhaps I was protecting Carlie.

Then there was Donald's son. In meetings that I was privy too, he would complain about Carlie's salary. She was making too much for her position. Donald Senior did not defend her. Did not communicate her longstanding loyalty. Did not once defy his son. Carlie had become a commodity, a liability, if he was to pursue a new relationship with Jill.

There was nothing I could do. I fed morsels to Carlie's soul. She was slowly being stripped of her authority and any power. She was surrendering without a fight. I did not know what it would take, but I believed in her.

"I have raised these kids like my own. I love them like my own."

"I know Carlie, but they don't deserve your love. They don't know any better. They are simply following the wishes of their twisted father. I know you find this hard to believe, but these meetings without you, Don Jr. thinks you are paid too much, you are dispensable. They are nothing like you Carlie."

She turned away. For an instant I thought I had lost her. She faced me once again with sadness in her blue eyes, with tenderness in her face. "I know it. I guess I've known it for a long time."

I knew one day Carlie would walk away with her head held high. Some people look powerless for such a long time. But just like I had been a long time ago, Carlie would break free. Some day the last thread of the spider web would be swept away. Some day she would wake up and say enough was enough. Every whisper in the leaves would be thunderous. Every bone in her body would scream. Carlie would not be waiting any longer.

As for myself, it was not going to happen yet, but I would be long gone before Carlie. My relationship with Donald became increasingly more difficult and confrontational. There would come a time when I could not stay out of his path, nor he of mine.

CHAPTER 56

THE DISAPPEARANCE

Winter had once again passed. The morning was pungent with spring air. There was no tinge of tiny green leaves emerging on the branches of poplar, no sprouts of early gooseberry. Only breaths and whispers of southerly wind that had gathered flavors of awakening balsam pine and the distinct scent of withering ice. Like an old ice cube that needs discarding. It would not be long now before my passage would be by boat, and not dogsled.

I loved this time of the year. The winters were long and harsh, leading to an amplified excitement to break free. It was a grand day. My Norwegian-style custom-made wooden kick sled was a good friend. With most of the snow having evaporated from the ice, my kick sled would glide easily, and Sekima was as eager as I to make the four-mile journey to town. In tougher conditions, I would have to help by kicking off with one leg, but today I stood on the back runners with a container of coffee to enjoy one of my near-last treks across the lake.

We were once again encapsulated by heavy fog, the warmer air meeting the ice. I could barely see in front of me. Unlike when I experienced fog in a boat, I felt comfortable. I was not going to run into a reef. I could see where snow machine tracks had left patterns notched into the ice. I trusted my companion, who had run this path many times before.

I hoped to be boating by the following week as the lake had turned its last coat of blemished white, its four or more feet of ice becoming rotted shards of needles. I could quite easily travel on two inches of good ice, when the ice first forms on the lake and temperatures continue to drop. Today, it was still likely two or more feet thick, but shorelines showed signs of water and hairline cracks gaped wide, with temperatures preventing any further ice-making. I crossed one, a hairline crack, an ice ridge, a mile or so away from home. It posed no problem. The open water cracks had once been ridges, large areas of ice being pushed together as the freezing water expanded with no place to go but upwards towards the heavens, crossing the lake like a winding zipper. Now the zippers had relaxed. The edges had fallen away from each other, gradually receding to shorelines with disappearing ice, sapphire water showing through like tiny streams crossing the expanse of ice. It was also an indication of where I was as they crisscrossed my path from north to south.

The fog was creepy, settling all around us. I had long since left the island, and there was nothing in sight. I heard them then. Off in the distance, their signature howl, a wolf pack on the move. They were communicating to each other, telling each other where they were. In the mist, it was impossible to say how close or far away they were as their call could be heard at long distances.

I bridged another open ridge, six inches to a foot of open water. The ice depth was substantial and visible below me. A minimum two feet of ice remained. Still, we knew it was deteriorating quickly, and we had already taken the truck onto mainland. The four-mile trek, with Sekima pulling at a paced trot, would take no more than twenty-five minutes.

The long howls reverberated around me. There was no wind. No direction. The fog was dense and endless. Another open ridge.

"Whoa." I called Sekima to a halt. The ridge had separated

between two and three feet. It wasn't daunting for dog or person to jump the gap, however, the knowledge that there was 150 feet of frigid water below us was troubling, especially with a malamute, harness, five feet of sled and a 125-pound woman bundled all together. I contemplated following the ridge to the north or south. Somewhere it would pull back together and be safe to cross. That, however, could be miles out of my way and lead me onto ice that I was not familiar with.

It was best to be safe, remove the harness on Sekima, let him jump the gap, and I would follow with the kick sled. The sled would not only bridge the gap but would distribute my weight. I was not about to make the same mistake twice.

Sekima's harness was made up of braided black nylon that looped over his broad shoulders and chest, running down his back and again looped at his thick glutes, preventing any shifting or rubbing. From there, the harness ran to either side of the front of the sled. The reins were separately attached to the harness, clipped on either side of his chest, and ran the full length of the sled to where I stood on the runners. I had to dismantle everything but his body harness, for fear that it would catch on a corner of the ice.

The wolf Pack sounded near; guttural sounds accompanied by barks that led me to believe they had made their kill. The fog was heavy, the sounds diluted and unevenly distributed, leaving me with no sense of their direction or distance.

Sekima stood alert, head tilted, nose to the air. If I'd had his nose, I would certainly have known the direction of the Pack. I tied his harness loosely on the sled and gave Sekima an urgent command.

"Let's go, Sekima. Go! Go!"

I watched him easily jump the span. I chose the same location to cross. I thrust hard with one leg at the last minute before bridging the gap and slid easily fifteen feet beyond before the sled rested. The fog spread completely around me. The vastness of the lake compressed into a small orbit that surrounded me. There was no sign of Sekima.

I heard them again. They were howling once more. The Pack was on the move. And so was Sekima, without me.

Follow the path. Do not let the fog distract you—push on or wait it out. I had been here before, at this exact moment in time and space. It was now my lone moment to make that decision. I had travelled this path many times with Sekima. I had travelled here with the Pack. We knew the course. We knew what waited ahead. If I veered my course, if I tried to find him, he would pick up my scent. He would keep going, believing that I was encouraging him to follow the wolves. The gravity of the moment penetrated deep within me. I had horrible images of what Sekima's final moments could be. They would not allow him to be part of their group, but he wouldn't know that. All those times of pure fear, of doubt, of peril – a meteor of flashing thoughts. Would he be true to us, or another Pack?

I kicked off with deliberation. I could hear them calling. I did not hesitate. I followed the course through the fog, and I could see Honeymoon Island ahead. Just like the time with the purple toboggan. Just like all the times before when we had found each other. Large, wolf-grey malamute – Sekima. He came running fast, extended strides, his front legs barely touching the crippled ice, his sinewy haunches pushing hard. He angled towards and ahead of me, knowing the path our Pack would take.

.

CPSIA information can be obtained
at www.ICGtesting.com
Printed in the USA
BVHW040633070822
643857BV00001B/9